The Enemy You Fear Fears You

The Enemy You Fear Fears You

There Is Power in Your Mouth

JOHN ADEBOLA

Foreword by Sunday Isehunwa

RESOURCE *Publications* · Eugene, Oregon

THE ENEMY YOU FEAR FEARS YOU
There Is Power in Your Mouth

Copyright © 2025 John Adebola. All rights reserved. Except for brief quotations in critical publications or reviews, no part of this book may be reproduced in any manner without prior written permission from the publisher. Write: Permissions, Wipf and Stock Publishers, 199 W. 8th Ave., Suite 3, Eugene, OR 97401.

Resource Publications
An Imprint of Wipf and Stock Publishers
199 W. 8th Ave., Suite 3
Eugene, OR 97401

www.wipfandstock.com

PAPERBACK ISBN: 979-8-3852-5903-8
HARDCOVER ISBN: 979-8-3852-5904-5
EBOOK ISBN: 979-8-3852-5905-2

09/26/25

To my late father, who laid the foundation of my faith—your life, your care, your generosity, and your unwavering commitment to family continue to inspire me every day.

Contents

Foreword by Sunday Isehunwa	ix
Preface	xi
Acknowledgments	xiii

PART I. THE WEAPONS OF THE DEVIL'S WARFARE

Chapter 1	The Invisible War	3
Chapter 2	Nature of the War	11
Chapter 3	The Devil's Weapons	19

PART II. KNOW YOUR ENEMY

Chapter 4	Recognize the Enemy	43
Chapter 5	Silence the Enemy and Avenger	52
Chapter 6	Secrets of Great Strength	61
Chapter 7	What of Fasting?	77

PART III. POWER IN YOUR MOUTH

Chapter 8	Power in Your Mouth	89
Chapter 9	Release the Power	94
Chapter 10	Why You Lost the Battle	114

Foreword

I AM THRILLED ABOUT the publication of this book and have been richly blessed by reading it. I have known the author for over three decades—as both a Christian and a servant of God—and I am delighted that he has shared insights drawn from a sound understanding of Scripture and real-life experience.

This book arrives at a time when conflicts abound—in personal lives, families, communities, and nations—while many remain unaware of what is truly happening, where things are headed, or how to respond to the surrounding chaos and find peace. Indeed, Jesus Christ foretold that conflict and warfare would intensify in the last days: "*And you will hear of wars and threats of wars, but don't panic. Yes, these things must take place, but the end won't follow immediately*" (Matthew 24:6, NLT). This book offers insight and clarity, revealing that behind many physical conflicts and wars lie unseen forces. It will greatly benefit anyone seeking to remain calm and victorious amid turmoil.

The author skillfully draws from Scripture to explain that the devil was originally created as Lucifer—meaning, "morning star," "day star," or "shining one"—a beautiful creation of God. However, through covetousness, he sought to usurp God's authority and elevate himself to equality with God. As a result, he fell from grace and became the great Dragon (a destroyer), the Serpent (a deceiver and liar), the Devil (a slanderer and instigator of evil), Satan (an adversary who opposes all that is good), the Accuser of the brethren, and the Avenger—though God declares, "Vengeance is mine" (Revelation 12:9–11; Psalm 8:2). Since Lucifer's fall, most wars and conflicts have stemmed from covetousness, the lusts of the flesh, the lust of the eyes, and the pride of life. Others arise from prayerlessness and the attempt to take God's role in human affairs (James 4:1–3).

Foreword

In this book, the author explains who our real enemy is, the nature of spiritual warfare, and the weapons the enemy commonly uses—such as ignorance, fear, and deception. Yet believers can overcome and silence the enemy and the avenger by cultivating spiritual strength and stamina, growing in the knowledge of God's word, walking in personal holiness, and defeating fear through faith, prayer, and fasting. We are also called to take proactive steps: confront and rebuke the devil when necessary, avoid unconfessed sin, and continually confess the victory Christ has secured for us through His blood (Revelation 12:11).

As you read this book, may you be strengthened, encouraged, and greatly blessed by God—just as Joseph and Jesus Christ triumphed over every challenge, attack, and scheme of the enemy (Genesis 49:22–26; Colossians 2:15).

Professor Sunday Isehunwa
University of Ibadan
Nigeria.

Preface

This book, an exposition of Psalm 8:2, has been in development for a long time. I wrote the initial draft and much of its content more than twenty years ago, which I have since updated with new insights and additional and relevant anecdotes from today.

There are three parts: First, it reveals the enemies and the Avenger—the devil—who are waging an invisible war. Second, this war targets all of humanity, particularly God's people. Third, we, as God's chosen warriors, are ordained by God to defeat or silence the Enemy and Avenger through our mouths. We are God's "babes and sucklings."

In Part I, I uncover the origin and scope of the war, its battlefield, how the devil and dark forces operate, and the foundation of our victory.

In Part II, I discuss how we believers, as the devil's primary targets, can protect ourselves and position for victory.

In Part III, I conclude by explaining how God has given us power through our mouths to overcome the forces of darkness—through faith confessions, praising Him, and prayer.

This revelation is simple yet profound and powerful. As Paul states in Galatians 1:12, I received this revelation not from any human but directly from the Holy Spirit.

This truth has deeply transformed me, revolutionizing my understanding of life and approach to spiritual warfare. The knowledge and practices shared in this book are ones I have tested and proven effective in my life, and I believe they will work for you because they are rooted in God's Word.

My prayer is that God will open your mind to grasp these truths. Through this book, I believe God will place power in your hands—power to take control of your life if the devil has been in charge.

Preface

By believing and applying the insights in this book, you can enter into rest from the devil's schemes. As Isaiah 10:27 (KJV) declares, "*. . . the yoke shall be destroyed because of the anointing.*" Amen and amen.

Acknowledgments

First and foremost, I give thanks to God Almighty, who, through the inspiration of His Holy Spirit, enabled me to write this book and has made its publication possible.

I am deeply grateful to Professor Sunday Isehunwa for generously taking time out of his demanding schedule to read the manuscript and provide a thoughtful and encouraging foreword.

Finally, I sincerely thank the endorsers of this book—Rev. Dr. Alexander Faranpojo, Dr. Sam Malomo, and Professor Sunday Isehunwa—for the confidence they have shown in me by contributing their kind endorsements.

PART I

THE WEAPONS OF THE DEVIL'S WARFARE

Chapter 1

The Invisible War

Most people go through life oblivious of the fact that they are involved in spiritual warfare. They do not understand that this world is a battlefield. Even most believers or born again Christians who know that there is a war going on do not understand the extent or the reality of this war. However, it is important that we know that there is a war and that the war is real. King David says in Psalm 8:2

> *Out of the mouth of babes and sucklings*
> *hast thou ordained strength because of thine enemies,*
> *that thou mightest still the enemy and the avenger*
> (KJV)

> *From the mouths and souls of infants and toddlers, the most innocent,*
> *You have decreed power to stop Your adversaries*
> *and quash those who seek revenge*
> (The Voice Bible)

The words *"enemies"* and *"enemy"* in the KJV translation highlights this reality. The word enemy implies hostility, opposition, conflict, battle, war, etc. Whenever there is an enemy, there will inevitably be antagonism and conflict.

Every human being is a combatant. You are either fighting on God's side or the devil's. There is no middle ground; you cannot be neutral. Nobody can sit on the fence, you are either actively or passively, directly or indirectly a combatant for God or for Satan, the archenemy.

PART I. THE WEAPONS OF THE DEVIL'S WARFARE

This spiritual war pits Satan, described in Psalm 8:2 as *"the Enemy and the Avenger"* against God. It is a battle between righteousness and unrighteousness, good and evil, light and darkness, originating in God's heaven before the world's creation. This conflict manifests in human affairs—through disputes, divisions, and relational strife. It fuels wars between nations and contributes to natural disasters like hurricanes, earthquakes, and tsunamis. The war is evident in heinous acts such as murders, including parents killing children and vice versa, friends killing friends, and senseless random violence. It also underlies moral decay, seen in adultery, sexual promiscuity, and deviant behaviors such as homosexuality, lesbianism, and other sexual perversions.

It began when Satan who was originally called Lucifer, which means the "morning star," or "day star" or "shining star" decided to usurp God's authority and to make himself equal to God. Satan expresses his rebellion and intentions in these verses:

How you have fallen from heaven,
O morning star, son of the dawn!
You have been cast down to the earth,
you who once laid low the nations!
You said in your heart,
"I will ascend to heaven;
I will raise my throne above the stars of God;
I will sit enthroned on the mount of assembly,
on the utmost heights of the sacred mountain.
I will ascend above the tops of the clouds;
I will make myself like the Most High."
Isaiah 14:12-14 (NIV)

The intentions of Lucifer are clear; he wanted to become like God. He, therefore, rebelled against God and secured the loyalty of one third of the angels in heaven to join him and he declared war on God. This rebellion is revealed in Revelations 12 where Satan was presented as the red dragon. In verse 4, it says, *"Its tail swept a third of the stars out of the sky and flung them to the earth . . ."* Stars in the Bible are sometimes used metaphorically to refer to angels. For example, Revelations 1:20 says, " . . . *The seven stars are the angels of the seven churches . . .*"

On a side note, you should know that the events of the Book of Revelation are not always in the future. Like the war in Heaven in Revelation 12:7, some of the events have already happened. In the book, Jesus was giving us a comprehensive view of related history, with most of it future but some are present, others are past.

Satan, described as the *"anointed cherub who covers"* (NKJV) or *"guardian cherub"* (NIV) in Ezekiel 28:14, may have believed his proximity to God granted him knowledge of divine power and secrets, leading him to imagine he could rival or equal God. As a chief angel, he might have enjoyed access to God that possibly surpassed even Archangels Michael or Gabriel. Ezekiel 28:14 (NIV) notes he was on the *"holy mountain"* and *"walked among the fiery stones,"* symbolizing God's abode and its sacred landscape. Yet, he was gravely mistaken. His rebellion failed, and God expelled him from the highest Heaven, the Heaven of heavens. Though Satan still occupies a lower heaven, he no longer dwells in God's presence.

Let me pause here and explain something. If you read Ezekiel 28 from verse 1, you will see that it was a prophecy about the king of Tyre. Therefore, you might wonder how verses 14 apply to Satan. This is how. Sometimes, the Bible addresses Satan or the demonic spirit possessing a human or that is at work through them, as though it is addressing the human.

One example is when Jesus admonished Peter for rebuking Him when He told them that He was going to be killed, and said to him *"Get behind Me, Satan! You are an offense to Me, for you are not mindful of the things of God, but the things of men."*—Matthew 16:23 (NKJV). Was Jesus saying that Peter was the devil? No, Jesus knew that Satan was the one speaking through Peter at that time. Therefore, he was addressing the devil who was speaking through him.

Another case is when Jesus confronted the Jews who wanted to kill Him, saying they were not God's children. He told them, *"You belong to your father, the devil, and you want to carry out his desires. He's been a murderer from the start . . . "* (John 8:44–45, NKJV).

The first murder and the first fratricide that occurred in human history was that of Abel by his brother Cain. We know that Cain murdered Abel but Jesus, pulling back the curtain, showed us that the devil was the mastermind and that Cain was the physical instrument that he used. The devil was the one who inspired and influenced Cain. Does saying that the devil was the mastermind absolve Cain of his responsibility for the murder? No. It is like in murder-for-hire cases, the perpetrator, (the person who actually committed the crime), is as guilty as or sometimes even more guilty than the mastermind. Cain's guilt is even more evident because God warned him not to do it when He told him " . . . *sin lies at the door. And its desire is for you, but you should rule over it"*—Genesis 4:7 (NIV). God told him to rule over it indicating that Cain had the power to say no to the devil but he did not. As Christian believers, we too do have the power to say no to sin.

We also see this in how Jesus sometimes addressed the demonic spirits at work in people. In Luke 8:26–39 where He encountered and healed the demon possessed man of Gadarenes. He asked him in verse 30 what his name was. It would appear that Jesus was speaking to the man but instead He was addressing the chief demon at work in the man, whose name was Legion.

Therefore, you can now see how although Ezekiel 28 appears to be talking of the king of Tyre, verses 13–15 was addressing Satan who was at work inside him. The king of Tyre could not possibly have done any of those things mentioned because they are celestial and non-human activities.

DIVINE PURPOSE IN CREATION

Following the rebellion of Satan, God decided to create the earth and to populate it with humans who He also chose to rule it. Genesis 1:26 expresses God's purpose as follows:

> *. . . let us make man in our image, in our likeness,*
> *and let them rule over the fish of the sea*
> *and the birds of the air, over the livestock, over all the earth,*
> *and over all the creatures that move along the ground.*
> (NIV)

God's purpose is striking because the devil rebelled, aiming to take control over God's creation, but God would not allow it. This shows us that God alone holds supreme authority. Nobody can claim power unless God appoints them. What is more, any authority established without God's blessing is invalid according to Heaven's laws, no matter how it looks on earth.

The Messengers in Daniel 4:17 announced that God humbled Nebuchadnezzar's arrogance so that " . . . *the living may know that the Most High is sovereign over the kingdoms of men and gives them to anyone he wishes and sets over them the lowliest of men."*—(NIV). After his restoration, Nebuchadnezzar himself acknowledged in verse 35 that *"He (God) does as he pleases with the powers of heaven and the peoples of the earth. No man can hold back his hand or say to him: what have you done?"* Hallelujah.

The devil had sought to seize control for himself but God preempted and humbled him. However, God in His good pleasure, decided to make humans ruler over His creation. The psalmist expresses this when he says:

> *You have made him ruler over the works of your hands;*
> *you put everything under his feet*
> Psalm 8:6 (NIV)

God chose to make humans rulers. So, understand this first: walking in dominion was not your idea or anyone else's—it came straight from God. If you believe this, it is yours to claim. No matter how much you have been oppressed, hurt, or afflicted, trust in this truth and God will make it real in your life. The zeal of the Lord will accomplish it. Amen.

Understand that your ability to walk in dominion does not stem from your own strength or power but from God's divine design. In Psalm 8:4, David marvels, "*What is mankind that you are mindful of them, human beings that you care for them?*" (NIV). Gazing at God's heavens—the moon, stars, and His mighty works—the psalmist ponders why God bestows such favor on humanity. This divine favor is precisely what has empowered you to live in dominion as God has ordained it.

That you can walk in dominion does not stem from your personal strength, wisdom, fervent prayer, or deep knowledge of God's Word, but primarily from God's divine favor. He desires for you to live in dominion. While praying and understanding Scripture are vital for this journey, they are not the foundation. Dominion is ultimately an act of God's sovereign grace, accessed through faith.

Many Christian believers are sick and oppressed even though they can and do pray, fast and know the Scripture. I believe that God will give you inspiring and life-changing insights through this book on how to be master over your circumstances and be in charge of your life.

If the devil has had you on the ropes and been in charge, God will put power in your hands through this book so that you can start to be in charge. You may have been oppressed and bruised for a long time by the devil, but God will arise on your behalf and overturn your captivity. Amen and amen. The Bible says, "*As they pass through the Valley of Baca, they make it a place of springs . . .* "—Psalm 84:6 (NIV). You may have been in the valley of Baca—"Baca" means weeping—but you are passing through and will pass through. Amen. Making it a place of springs means that God wants you to learn from the valley experience and share it with others.

PART I. THE WEAPONS OF THE DEVIL'S WARFARE

DEVIL'S ENMITY

The devil was furious that God picked humans— frail and humble humans—to rule over His creation. He was jealous that God favored humans above angels. Therefore, he decided to attack God by targeting humanity. Having learned from his own rebellion that he could not challenge God directly, he figured striking at humans would hurt God. Thus, he launched a war against humankind, tempting Adam and Eve in the Garden of Eden, leading to their fall. Ever since that moment, the devil has waged a relentless campaign to pull humanity away from godliness toward ungodliness, from righteousness to unrighteousness, and from light into darkness.

The devil has largely succeeded. The Bible says "*. . . the whole world is under the control of the evil one*"—1 John 5:19 (NIV). He has succeeded considerably because of a campaign of deception that he has carried on. Our Lord Jesus says "*. . . there is no truth in him. When he lies, he speaks his native language, for he is a liar and the father of lies*"—John 8:44 (NIV). The devil's enmity is the root cause of the conflicts and challenges we observe in the world today.

You may have faced troubles in your life and longed for a life free from them—I understand. I once felt that way and sometimes still do. However, I want you to realize that challenges are a natural part of life, stemming sometimes from the devil's enmity. In Matthew 7, Jesus concludes the Sermon on the Mount with the analogy of a house built on rock versus on sand, illustrating those who follow His teachings versus those who do not. As He states in verse 25, "*. . . the rain descended, the floods came, and the winds blew and beat on that house*" for both. Believers and unbelievers alike face life's storms, but whether we triumph or falter depends on whether we have God on our side or not.

In addition, it is often through challenging or negative experiences that we come to truly discover ourselves—both our strengths and our weaknesses. They deepen our understanding of the human condition and help clarify how others perceive us, including their motivations and intentions. When we handle them wisely, such experiences can become opportunities to build both spiritual and emotional resilience. As (Proverbs 24:10 NKJV) says, "*If you faint in the day of adversity, your strength is small.*"

The Lord Jesus said, "*I have told you these things, so that in Me you may have peace. In this world you will have trouble. But take heart! I have overcome the world*" (John 16:33, NIV). Therefore, you can take comfort in the confident assurance that Jesus has already overcome on your behalf—and because of Him, you too will overcome.

Troubles, though unpleasant, are beneficial to our spiritual health. God allows them in our lives to strengthen our spiritual resilience. He does not intend for us to remain weak or immature in our faith. Rather, He is training us—as seen in Judges 3:1–3—so that we can fight our own battles, assist others in theirs, and engage faithfully in the battles of the Lord.

God told the serpent, that is the devil in Genesis 3:15 *"I will put enmity between you and the woman, and between your offspring and hers . . ."* but He also promised, *". . . he [the seed of the woman who is Jesus] will crush your head and you [the serpent or Satan] will strike his heel."*

Satan struck the heel of Jesus through the crucifixion. Jesus alluded to this when, quoting Psalm 41:9, He said in John 13:18, *"He who eats bread with Me has lifted up his heel against Me."* Yet by His death on the cross and His resurrection, Jesus crushed the serpent's head, fulfilling the promise of Genesis 3:15. And because you are included in Christ, you too will crush the head of the serpent. Amen and amen.

THE HUMAN TRAP

The devil has deceived humanity by claiming that serving God is enslavement, that we are not free, and that God is a tyrant. He falsely asserts that God's righteous laws violate human liberties. This is the devil's most profound and sinister lie. This is why the kings and rulers in Psalm 2:3 declare, *"Let us break their [God and His Anointed One] chains,"* and proclaim, *"and throw off their shackles."* The use of *"chains"* and *"shackles"* suggests that we are God's captives, trapped in bondage.

Humanity has largely believed this lie, which explains the rampant lawlessness we see in the world today. People believe that obeying God's laws robs them of their freedom and in their pursuit of liberty, they indulge in all forms of unrighteousness.

However, Jesus says in John 8:34 that *" . . . everyone who sins is a slave to sin."* We are not free if we live in sin; we are instead in bondage. We are only and truly free when we live for God. A lot of men and women today are bound by ungodly habits and practices: alcohol, sex, drugs, cheating, lying, occultism, smoking, anger, etc.

At first, it might have felt thrilling and liberating. Perhaps people pursued these things seeking freedom, but now they face the harsh truth of their enslavement. Many are now desperate for deliverance. If you are among them, know that Jesus can set you free. You may not have realized you are in bondage, but if you are living in sin, you are enslaved to sin and the devil.

To find freedom, simply believe in your heart that Jesus died for you and rose again, and invite Him into your life as your Lord and Savior. Romans 10:9 says that

> *If you confess with your mouth 'Jesus is Lord'*
> *and believe in your heart that God raised him from the dead,*
> *you will be saved*
> (NIV)

If you sincerely desire to turn from a life of sin, and pray according to this scripture, the power of God will come upon you, break the power of sin over your life, and destroy the desire for ungodliness.

It is only when we live according to the laws of God, that we are truly free. James describes God's laws as the "*. . . law of liberty . . .*" James 1:25. It is the law of God that gives freedom. It is in your best interest that you live according to God's law doing what is right and pleasing to God. As a Christian believer, you cannot walk in dominion if you live in sin. The Bible says "*. . . a man is a slave to whatever has mastered him*"—2 Peter 2:19 (NIV).

Anyone who lives in sin is a servant of the devil. In fact, the Bible says, "*He who does what is sinful is of the devil, because the devil has been sinning from the beginning.*"—1 John 3:8. If you are a born again believer, you must understand that the liberty we have in Christ is not "*to indulge the sinful nature*"—Galatians 5:13—or to be used "*as a cover-up for evil*"—1 Peter 2:16.

I mentioned earlier that this war is between righteousness and unrighteousness, and between light and darkness. God wants us to live holy but the devil wants us to live in dishonesty, stealing, lying, covetousness, murder, adultery, fornication, hatred, envy, etc. This is why the devil has declared war on humanity and his objective is to turn us against God and His righteous requirements.

To prevail in this spiritual war, you must understand its nature and the devil's tactics. I will explore these in the next chapter.

Chapter 2

Nature of the War

THIS WAR IS NOT physical; it is spiritual. It is organized in the heavens by the hosts of darkness but conducted on earth against humanity. Believers are the primary targets of these attacks because we have changed camps—from the camp of the devil to the camp of God and have resolved to live for God.

This is what has earned us—believers—the wrath and bitter enmity of the devil. The Bible says that God has "... *delivered us the power of darkness, and hath translated us into the kingdom of his dear son [the Lord Jesus]*"—Colossians 1:13 (KJV).

This battle is not physical but spiritual because we are not fighting against physical forces but against spiritual forces. Apostle Paul says:

> *For we wrestle not against flesh and blood,*
> *but against principalities, against powers,*
> *against the rulers of the darkness of this world,*
> *against spiritual wickedness in high places*
> Ephesians 6:12 (KJV)

Paul again says, "*For though we walk in the flesh, we do not war after the flesh*"—2 Corinthians 10:3 (KJV). Although we are human beings, we are not fighting against physical enemies or forces but against spiritual forces.

PART I. THE WEAPONS OF THE DEVIL'S WARFARE

BELIEVERS VICTORY

In this spiritual war, only born-again believers—those who have accepted Jesus as their Lord—can come out victorious. Scripture declares in 1 John 5:4–5 (NIV):

For everyone born of God overcomes the world.
This is the victory that has overcome the world, even our faith.
Who is it that overcomes the world?
Only he who believes that Jesus is the Son of God

If you are born of God, you can live in victory. You have been given the power to overcome because God's seed is in you (1 John 3:9). That is the key to your triumph. God's seed is like His spiritual DNA, a part of His nature planted in you, making you part of His family. Biologically, having a favorable or the "right" DNA drives your immune system to resist and combat some diseases and infections. Similarly, God's seed equips you to overcome sickness and the devil's schemes. It is God's very life within you, empowering you to walk in authority and dominion.

Many identify as "Christians," attend church regularly or occasionally and affiliate with various Christian denominations, but are they truly Christians or believers? Not necessarily. I grew up in a devout Anglican household where faith shaped our lives. My father, a committed Christian, ensured we attended church every Sunday, and my siblings and I faithfully went to Sunday school. At home, we prayed together each morning and evening, and Bible reading was a regular practice. Yet, for all this, I was not truly a Christian or a believer. My family's or even my father's faith could not make me one.

A true Christian is someone who has confessed, "Jesus is the Son of God," not merely as words but as a deeply held belief reflected in their actions. During the Apostles' time, Jesus' disciples were first called members of the "Way" and later Christians in Antioch (Acts 11:26). A disciple follows the teachings of Jesus and the Bible. Being born of God or born again means relying wholly on Jesus for justification and salvation, not in venerating, or praying to, religious icons or the so-called "saints," or in performing empty sacraments not ordained by Jesus, as some do. Jesus told us to pray only to the Father and in His name—John 16:23–24. Have you committed your life to Jesus and live for Him? Do you have the Holy Spirit's witness in your heart, confirming you are God's child (Romans 8:16)? Only those who believe in this manner and possess this inner witness are true Christians.

Nature of the War

Believing that Jesus is the Son of God is not just a mental acknowledgment but also a living experience. If you have not been born again, you cannot overcome; you are still under the dominion of darkness and under the power of the devil.

This victory is not for everyone because it is only the cross and the blood of Jesus that procures, ensures, and secures victory over the devil and his demonic hosts. The Bible says that Jesus has "... *disarmed the powers and authorities, he made a public spectacle of them, triumphing over them by the cross*"—Colossians 2:15 (NIV). It is because of this triumph of Jesus that we who are born again can triumph over the forces of darkness.

In Revelations chapter 12, after the Archangel Michael cast the great dragon, Satan and his angels out of heaven, a voice spoke in heaven of the victory of believers saying:

> *... they overcame him by the blood of the Lamb*
> *and by the word of their testimony;*
> *they did not love their lives*
> *so much as to shrink from death*
> Revelations 12:11 (NIV)

They overcame by three things: One, by the blood of the Lamb. Two, by the word of their testimony. Three, by not loving their lives so much as to shrink from death. Let us unpack each of these one by one:

1. The first key to victory is overcoming through the "*blood of the Lamb.*" This means you must be a born-again believer to share in the victory of the cross, reserved only for those redeemed and cleansed by Jesus' blood. Apostle John writes, "*Everyone born of God overcomes the world. This is the victory that has overcome the world—our faith*" (1 John 5:4, NIV). That is faith in Jesus Christ. Without being born again, you have no hope of winning life's battles—you are defenseless and vulnerable. However, by surrendering your life to God and becoming born again, you can start overcoming.

2. The second key to overcoming the devil is the "*word of their testimony.*" What you say matters greatly for living in victory. You might stay defeated because of negative or wrong confessions. Your words carry power. Speak God's Word over your situation. Stop saying negative things about your life and you will start walking in victory.

3. The third key is that "*they did not love their lives*" so much as to shy away from death; they were ready to die for their faith and, in some cases,

actually laid down their lives for it. Many of us may not face death or persecution for our faith, but we often demonstrate that we love ourselves more than we love the Lord or that we value our lives more than our faith through self-indulgence. Some men prioritize sports over their spiritual health. Women focus more on the latest fashion trends and shopping than their spiritual well-being. People dedicate hours to video or online games; they spend hours on social media but struggle to spend an hour reading and studying the Bible or praying. Living in bitterness, envy, unforgiveness, lust, anger, or similar sins prevents us from walking in victory. Some Christians endure severe oppression—barrenness, depression, or affliction—because they refuse to forgive those who wronged them. Unforgiveness places you in the hands of *"tormentors"* (Matthew 18:34—KJV). Let me elaborate. In Matthew 18:21–34, Jesus shares the parable of the unforgiving servant, who, despite been forgiven a great debt by his master, refused to forgive his fellow servant. As a result, the master handed him over to the *"tormentors."* Similarly, when we withhold forgiveness from those who seek it, we risk forfeiting God's protection and grace, leaving ourselves vulnerable to demonic attacks. These *"tormentors"* represent demonic forces that can oppress believers. Despite fervent prayer, fasting, and confessing God's Word, some believers remain afflicted, sick, or oppressed, their circumstances unchanged, often because unforgiveness opens the door to such spiritual attacks. Others face oppression in their dreams, such as sexual encounters, because they harbor lust. They feed their lust by consuming pornographic or sexually immoral movies and TV shows, reading indecent literature, or listening to immoral music. These choices keep them bound. Though they may have fasted, prayed, and received prayers from anointed ministers, their yokes remain unbroken.

Victory over Condemnation

One of Satan's schemes is to convince believers that they cannot walk in victory because they are not forgiven, not living righteously, or have somehow fallen out of God's favor. He often brings false accusations, making God's people feel condemned for things they did not do or of which they are not truly guilty. Apostle Paul says in Romans 8:1, *"There is therefore now no condemnation to those who are in Christ Jesus . . .* " You must learn to recognize and overcome this tactic.

I will explore Satan's schemes more fully in Chapter 3, but for now, let me address one of his common deceptions—the false condemnation that you are "*walking in unforgiveness*" simply because you have not forgiven someone who hurt you and has not asked for forgiveness, or because you still remember what they did. Revelation 12:10 does not call him the "*accuser of our brethren*" for nothing. So let us turn to the Word of God.

You may have heard the phrase "*forgive and forget*" preached, suggesting we should automatically forgive someone who wrongs us, but that is not what the Bible teaches. Scripture never says we must automatically forgive. Instead, Jesus teaches that we should forgive when someone who has wronged us asks for forgiveness or shows repentance. Forgiveness comes as a response to their request.

In Jesus' teaching on forgiveness in Matthew 18:21–35, when Peter asked Him in verse 21 if he should only forgive someone who has wronged him up to seven times, Jesus said no but up to seventy times seven times, that is four hundred and ninety times (490). Jesus was effectively saying that there is no limit to how many times we should forgive someone. However, He also told the parable of the unmerciful servant to illustrate the condition under which we should forgive.

The king forgave the servant when he asked his forgiveness but the servant did not grant the same grace to his fellow servant who asked his forgiveness. Forgiveness is to be granted whenever someone acknowledges their wrong against us and asks our forgiveness. It is when we do not forgive in response to someone asking our forgiveness that we are living in unforgiveness.

However, you may choose, of your own free will, to forgive someone who has wronged you even if they have not asked for your forgiveness—just as Jesus did on the cross when He forgave those who tortured and crucified Him. Another example is Stephen, one of the seven deacons, who in Acts 7:60 forgave his killers as he was dying. However, the Bible does not require you to forgive someone who has not asked your forgiveness and it is not unforgiveness if you are not there yet. It is unforgiveness only if you refuse after they have asked you. Jesus taught this in Luke 17:3–4 when He said this,

> *If your brother or sister sins against you, rebuke them;*
> *and if they repent, forgive them.*

PART I. THE WEAPONS OF THE DEVIL'S WARFARE

Even if they sin against you seven times in a day and seven times
come back to you saying 'I repent,'
you must forgive them.
(NIV)

Notice that Jesus says we must forgive only if they come back each time and ask our forgiveness. Besides, in John 20:23, Jesus states, "*If you forgive the sins of any, they are forgiven them; if you retain the sins of any, they are retained.*" Notice that Jesus indicates we may choose to retain sins. You might argue that this applies specifically to the church or the collective body of believers rather than to individuals. That may be true, but it still suggests that we are not obligated to forgive every sin—particularly when the one who wronged us has not sought forgiveness.

To illustrate this point further, consider examples from the Apostles. In 1 Timothy 1:20, Apostle Paul refers to Hymenaeus and Alexander, stating, "*. . . whom I delivered to Satan that they may learn not to blaspheme.*" In 2 Timothy 4:14, Paul, likely speaking of the same Alexander, notes that he caused him significant harm, declaring, "*. . . May the Lord repay him according to his deeds.*" Alexander, who opposed God's work and Paul personally (verse 15), showed no repentance or sought forgiveness. Consequently, Paul did not extend forgiveness for their blasphemy and opposition to God's mission.

Another example is Apostle Jude, who in Jude 1:11 pronounces, "*Woe to them!*" against those corrupting the church with false teachings, greed, sexual immorality, and division. He further declares in verse 13 that they are destined for "*the blackness of darkness forever.*" These individuals, though appearing as believers, were false in their faith. Were Paul and Jude harboring unforgiveness? Certainly not. Their stance reflects righteous judgment against unrepentant opposition to God's truth by unrepentant individuals who are not sorry for their wrongdoing.

We should forgive someone who wrongs us each time they ask for forgiveness but it is not unforgiveness if you hold off when they have not sought your pardon. Also, although we are not required to forgive if someone has not asked, we should still strive to forgive. Unforgiveness is emotional baggage that can weigh you down and eventually lead to bitterness, resentment, or even hatred—none of which are good for your spiritual or emotional well-being.

Forgiveness—especially when the offense is severe—can be a complex and deeply personal process. People have different levels of grace, and sometimes they need space to work through their emotions. Teaching that believers must automatically forgive even when the offender has not asked for forgiveness can be unhelpful and even damaging—it is frankly not biblical. I want you to understand that if someone has hurt you and has not sought your forgiveness—or if you are still healing and processing your emotions—you are not walking in unforgiveness. Working through pain takes time, and God, who sees the heart, is patient and compassionate through that process. If you are struggling to forgive someone, consider speaking honestly with someone you trust. Sharing your burden can help you begin to process your emotions and move toward emotional freedom.

Also, on the forget part of "forgive and forget," you should definitely not forget because you need to remember it to inform your future relationship with that person. For example, if you lent someone some money, he or she did not pay you back but asked your forgiveness, and you forgave him or her as the Bible says that you should, it would be foolish of you to lend him or her money again in the future given his or her past performance.

Your past experience with them should serve as a lesson, as most people, sadly, do not change. Does this mean that you should never lend them money in the future if you are able to? Not necessarily, but it should depend on your judgment of their character and performance since the last time you loaned them money. Alternatively, instead of lending, you might choose to give the money as a gift, if you are able, to avoid expecting repayment.

You may also have heard or been told that if you avoid someone who has wronged you and has not apologized and do not speak to them, that you are walking in or keeping malice. People who say or believe this do not know what malice means. The Merriam-Webster dictionary defines malice as,

desire to cause pain, injury, or distress to another
Or
intent to commit an unlawful act or cause harm without legal justification or excuse.

By these definitions, simply not speaking to someone is not malice unless you harbor evil intentions toward them or plan to and/or actually do them harm. You might avoid conversation because it always leads to conflict or shouting matches, or because they are unreasonable, making silence the wiser choice. It could also be that they do not want to talk, and you must respect their wishes. As Christians, we should strive to resolve disputes, but only as far as possible, for the Bible says, *"If it is possible, as much as depends on you, live peaceably with all men"*—Romans 12:18 (NKJV).

I have taken this brief detour to clarify what unforgiveness truly means, as there is often confusion around it. Satan frequently uses this misunderstanding to trap believers with thoughts of guilt and condemnation, making them feel they are *"walking in unforgiveness."* If you have ever felt that way—or are feeling that way now—I pray that you find freedom through a right understanding of what forgiveness really is.

Making the people of God feel condemned for things God does not condemn is one of the devil's schemes. I will explore more of these schemes in the next chapter.

Chapter 3

The Devil's Weapons

We often hear or teach what Apostle Paul says in 2 Corinthians 10:4: "*. . . the weapons of our warfare are not carnal but mighty through God for pulling down strongholds.*" God has given us the powerful weapons that Paul lists in Ephesians 6:13–18 to battle the forces of darkness. These we are aware of and often hear about. Yet, we often fail to understand or discern that the devil also has his weapons of warfare that he uses against us. Knowing how to counter these weapons is crucial to prevailing in spiritual warfare.

The troubling reality that exists in the church today is that many of God's people are defeated, overwhelmed, wounded, afflicted, and oppressed. However, this is not due to any lack of divine provision for our victory, as Scripture clearly declares, "*for everyone born of God overcomes the world*" (1 John 5:4, NIV) and "*. . . we are more than conquerors through him who loved us*" (Romans 8:37, NIV).

In addition, this is not because our liberty in Christ is not real for the Scripture says "*who [Jesus] hath delivered us from the powers of darkness . . .*"—Colossians 1:13 (KJV). We are indeed free because Apostle Paul again says in Galatians 5:1 (KJV), "*Stand fast therefore in the liberty wherewith Christ hath made us free . . .* " Jesus, Himself said, " *. . . if the Son sets you free, you will be free indeed*"—John 8:36 (NIV).

Despite these promises and provisions, many of God's people are not living in freedom, and their experiences seem to challenge or contradict these truths. Yet, the promises remain true and reliable, for as Jesus said, "*. . . Scripture cannot be broken . . .* "—John 10:35 (NKJV). Amen. God has

PART I. THE WEAPONS OF THE DEVIL'S WARFARE

also equipped us for victory and liberty by providing His armor—Ephesians 6:12.

Why then are most of God's people not free from satanic control and are always needing deliverance and healing? I believe the answer lies in this verse:

> *Put on the full armor of God*
> *so that you can take your stand*
> *against the devil's schemes.*
> Ephesians 6:11

Apostle Paul, inspired by the Holy Spirit, says to put on the whole armor of God that "*. . . you may be able to stand against the schemes of the devil*" (ESV). Notice that it does not say to stand directly against the demonic authorities, powers, rulers, or the wicked spirits in heavenly places who are our enemies—but rather, to stand against the devil's schemes. This distinction is crucial for understanding how to triumph over the forces of darkness. It reveals that by overcoming the devil's schemes, you overcome these forces.

The devil has no new scheme; it is the same old plan. Therefore, if you understand his schemes, then you can overcome him in your own life. It is very important that we know and understand the schemes of the devil if we must win in our battles against him.

Through an understanding revealed to me by the Holy Spirit, I have concluded: *spiritual warfare is won by revealed knowledge.* You must understand the truth about the devil—his limited power, schemes, and operations. Equally, you need to know your covenant rights, the guarantees of your liberty, the power of the blood, the name of Jesus, and the Word of God. Without this knowledge, you will not be in a position to prevail.

It is important to understand that Ephesians 6:11 tells us to put on the full armor of God—not to confront the hierarchy of demonic hosts directly, but to stand against the devil's schemes. *This distinction—standing against the schemes rather than directly against the demonic powers—is critical for prevailing in spiritual warfare.* As I mentioned earlier, when we overcome these schemes, we prevent the powers of darkness from defeating us.

I am convinced that many of God's people fall under demonic influence due to a lack of understanding about how the devil wages war and the schemes he employs. *These schemes are the weapons he uses to assault both believers and humanity at large.* Ignorance of these schemes gives the devil a significant advantage, leaving us vulnerable to his attacks. So, let us consider what a scheme is. A scheme is variously defined as:

A systematic plan of action
Or
A secret or devious plan; a plot
Or
An orderly plan or arrangement of related parts
(The American Heritage Dictionary)

One thing that is clear from all these definitions is that *a scheme is a plan*, systematic, secret, devious, and orderly. The devil has a plan to deprive the people of God of the freedom that we have in Christ and to keep us in bondage. It is a plan devised and prepared in the secret places of demonic forces.

A scheme is also systematic and methodical. A system is among others "*an organized or established procedure.*" Generally, a system is an organized set of interconnected components that work together to achieve a purpose. It may involve procedures, persist over time, and operate consistently. *Disrupting the system, in whole or part, would prevent it from producing the intended results.*

The devil and his demonic forces operate through a well-established and organized system. Their methods are persistent, recursive, and repetitive. This system is ancient—the devil has used the same tactics throughout all of human history. He has no new schemes. Therefore, when you understand how his schemes work and disrupt even one part of them, you disrupt the entire system. This knowledge is essential for our victory as believers.

Sun Tzu, a Chinese general who is considered one of the foremost military thinkers and strategists in history famously wrote in The Art of War: "*If you know yourself but not the enemy, for every victory gained you will also suffer a defeat.*" If you are ignorant of the devil's schemes and tactics, you leave yourself vulnerable to defeat.

The devil uses many schemes, and I want to share with you some key insights the Lord has revealed to me about the *major ones*. These schemes are cunning tricks and tactics the devil uses to strip God's people of their liberty and control their lives. In the pages that follow, you will gain understanding of these deceptive tactics and discover the powerful authority God has given you to overcome them. Read on to uncover the enemy's strategies—and learn how to defeat them.

PART I. THE WEAPONS OF THE DEVIL'S WARFARE

WEAPON OF FEAR

I am convinced that the devil's greatest scheme by which he controls and oppresses people's lives is with fear. Not all fear is evil because the Bible says, *"The fear of the Lord is the beginning of wisdom . . . "*—Proverbs 9:10 (NIV). However, any fear that takes away your courage, makes you anticipatory of evil, and makes you feel apprehensive and insecure is a satanically induced fear. This is the fear that I am talking about.

Any fear that does not inspire respect for and obedience to God is not of God, it is of the devil. This includes the fear of another human being. The Scripture clearly says that that we should not be afraid of any human being. In fact, the Bible says that the *"Fear of man will prove to be a snare . . . "*—Proverbs 29:25 (NIV).

As a Christian, if you are afraid of another human being, you will not be able to obey God, as you should. The devil will use that fear to ensnare you and get you to do what you should not do. If the three Hebrew young men: Shadrach, Meshach and Abednego had been afraid of Nebuchadnezzar, the devil would have ensnared them into Babylonian idolatry.

In 1 John 5:19, the Bible says, *"We know that we are children of God, and that the whole world is under the control of the evil one."* Some years ago, the Holy Spirit told me that one of the ways the devil has been able to bring the world under his power, is with fear.

Fear is one of the devil's strongest weapons. Almost everyone battles some kind of fear. I have learned there are over a thousand fears that grip people—fear of death, accidents, crime, or sickness; fear of the unknown or what is ahead; fear of darkness or night; fear of heights, flying, or sea travel; fear of animals, the occult, failure, and so much more.

There is a kind of fear I believe is natural and God-given. This fear, which helps you avoid danger, is like an in-built safety switch from God to protect you from harm. For instance, you should not fear electricity just because it exists, but if you spot a live wire and avoid touching it to escape a shock, that is just good sense. You should not fear things like snakes, lizards, cats, dogs, cockroaches, or bugs just for being what they are.

I have said that any fear that makes you expect the worst—like fearing you'll be a victim of crime—or any fear that leaves you rattled, uneasy, or anxious, comes from the devil. It does not matter what it is about; that kind of fear is demonic and a spirit. Scripture tells us, *"God has not given us a spirit of fear . . . "* (2 Timothy 1:7, NKJV). You need to know that this fear I am talking about is a spirit sent to torment you.

As a young believer, I used to brush off fear, pretending it was just a fleeting feeling or emotion that would pass. However, it would stick around, refusing to leave. Back then, I did not realize it was a demonic spirit I needed to resist and cast out. You have to understand this truth to overcome your fear and defeat it for good.

The *spirit of fear* is a spirit that binds and controls you. Do not let this fear take root in your life, or the devil will use it to trap you in bondage and rule over you. Scripture says Jesus defeated the devil, who holds the power of death, and freed us " . . . *who through fear of death were all their lifetime subject to bondage*" (Hebrews 2:14–15, NKJV).

I want you to notice that it says they were held in bondage through fear—specifically, the fear of death. A minister once shared the story of a woman whom God delivered through his ministry. For many years before her deliverance, she lived shut away in her room, completely isolated from human contact, all because of fear. She would only open her door briefly to receive food.

Some people avoid things like eating certain foods, dining at others' homes, wearing specific colors, visiting certain places, flying, or shaking hands. They do not skip these things because they dislike them or think they are wrong—they are driven by fear that something bad might happen. That kind of fear is a trap, chaining them in bondage.

A year before I became a born-again believer in 1987, I went through a prolonged illness that seemed to resist every form of medication. During that time, the devil whispered to me that I had an incurable disease and that I was going to die. As a result, I developed a deep and overwhelming fear of death.

The fear was so overwhelming that it bound and controlled me. Back then, whenever it got dark and I knew that bedtime was approaching, I became terrified. I might have been happy and excited before then, but immediately my mood changes and I become sad. It may not be apparent to those around me but it is on my inside.

At night, I will not sleep at all. I will just lie on my bed and gaze at the ceiling. I will not even dare to close my eyes because I believe that I would die if I were to fall asleep. That continued for many days until after some time, it subsided. However, it did not completely go away but remained dormant within me. When I looked back over it, one mistake I made was that I did not share it with anyone. Even though I was staying with my older sister and husband who are both believers and mature Christians, I never shared it with them. If you are disturbed by fear, please share it with someone who can help you.

A few years after I became born again, I experienced a severe attack from the devil that reawakened that fear of death. The attack lasted for at least four hours without stopping, during which the devil repeatedly told me he was going to kill me. However, through persistent prayer—both mine and my family's—God prevailed. Subsequently, I found the relevant truths and as I began to meditate and fix my mind and heart on them, the power of God's Word destroyed the fear.

I prayed for God to free me from every fear I had, and He did. No matter what fear grips you, God can set you free. The devil still tries to scare me at times, but now that I know fear is a spirit, I handle it by speaking God's Word, just like Jesus did during His temptation in the wilderness, and by casting that spirit out. Faith in the Word of God is the antidote to fear.

The Enemy You Fear

Let me share another revelation on the topic of fear that will help you to overcome your fears. As I previously noted, fear is a tool and weapon of the devil; it is a scheme by which the devil controls people's lives. So, one of the things you must do to prevail in the fight with the forces of darkness is to overcome your fear. Every soldier must learn to overcome their fears before they go into battle. You must fight to secure the victory that is already yours. I discussed this in detail later. Oftentimes however, believers live in fear of their enemies and are therefore afraid to fight. They feel impotent and feel paralyzed by fear.

When I was in my early twenties and doing graduate studies, I had an experience that I both regret and am proud of because it was a watershed event, a turning point in my life. I had a very close and dear friend who lived in the same graduate resident hall (dorm) as I. One day, while visiting this friend of mine, he had a dispute with a roommate who had powerful connections with what is called in the US, Resident Assistant (RA) and the hall Warden. The Warden is a senior university faculty member, usually a professor, appointed by the university to oversee a given hall.

I do not remember now what the dispute was about but this resident got the RA involved and eventually the Warden. One of the connections between these three individuals was that they belonged to the same religion; they were Muslims. Although Muslims generally were in the minority on campus, this Warden was a powerful professor who students feared greatly and widely and who was hostile to Christian believers. Wardens were extremely powerful and could revoke your residency or punish you in some other ways.

This roommate was clearly at fault, but with connections, he lied to the RA and Warden about the dispute. The Warden entered our room and asked my friend for his version of events. Upset and scared of possible consequences, my friend shared what really happened, then looked to me to back him up. However, I froze, too terrified of the Warden to speak a word in his defense.

The issue eventually was sorted out, but it weighed on me for a while. I felt ashamed and upset that I would let my friend down, too scared of another person to speak up for him. We never talked about it later, but it troubled me deeply, so I decided to act. I began praying for God to free me from fearing people—any person. God answered, and now I am never afraid to stand up for others or myself no matter who is in front of me or what their status is. My boldness is so strong now that some people mistake it for arrogance, but it is really just confidence rooted in trusting God.

Gideon's Truth

It was partly from this experience that God taught me a powerful truth and lesson about not being afraid of any human. One of the ways God taught me this is through the story of Gideon in Judges Chapter 7.

God had called Gideon to deliver the Israelites from the power of the Midianites who had oppressed them for 7 years. The Midianites were so oppressive and the Israelites were so demoralized that they hid in dens, caves and strongholds in the mountains—Judges 6:2. In fact, when the angel appeared to Gideon, Gideon was threshing wheat in a winepress. Wheat is normally threshed on a threshing floor.

Gideon was afraid because, as he said, he was from Manasseh, which was the weakest clan of Israel and was the least in his father's house—Judges 6:15 but he was doubly afraid because of the Midianites. He was eventually persuaded by the angel to accept his calling but he was still very fearful. Therefore, to build up his confidence, he asked God to prove to him that He was going to deliver the Israelites by his hands through a series of tests. Some of the tests include the wet and dry wool fleece tests that you would be familiar with—Judges 6:36-40.

In spite of all these proofs, Gideon was still very much afraid to go to battle against the Midianites. Finally, God told him to go to the camp of the Midianites and hear what they were saying. He went down with his servant where he overheard one Midianite soldier telling another a dream that he had—Judges 7:13-14. In the dream, he saw a loaf of barley bread strike their tent, overturn it and caused the tent to collapse. The other soldier told him that it symbolizes the sword of Gideon and meant that God will deliver the Midianites into his hands.

God said to me *"The enemy you fear, fears you."* The enemy you are afraid of is, in fact, afraid of you. Here Gideon was afraid of the Midianites but the Midianites were actually afraid of him. The Midianites camped opposite the Israelites by the hill of Moreh and were numerically superior to them but did not attack because they were afraid. Typically, an army launches an offensive when confident in its numerical or tactical superiority, or when better equipped than its adversary. The Midianites, with their numerically superior forces, may or may not have noticed Israel's army dwindle from 32,000 to 10,000, and finally to just 300 men. However, despite their advantage in numbers and weaponry, they hesitated to attack because they too were paralyzed by fear.

As believers, our confidence also comes from numerical strength and superior resources, akin to manpower and advanced weaponry. Let me elaborate on this.

There is a story in 2 Kings Chapter 6 where the king of Syria sent an army to capture Prophet Elisha. The reason is that Elisha has been revealing his battle plans to the king of Israel. This perplexed him and he initially thought that they had a mole among them. His commanders and advisers then told him that Elisha was the one behind the leak.

During the night, the Syrian army took positions around the city where Elisha was. When Elisha's servant woke up in the morning and saw that the city was surrounded, he was very afraid. However, Elisha knowing better, said to him " . . . *those who are with us are more than those who are with them"*—verse 16—and then prayed that God will open the servant's spiritual eyes. God did and the servant saw that the army of God's angels was bigger than the Syrian army surrounding the city.

As a believer, you need to know that you have a bigger army of angels protecting and fighting for you than any enemy that you can see or not see. The Bible says " . . . *He who is in you is greater than he who is in the world"*—1 John 4:4 (NKJV). He who is in us is Jesus; the one who is in the world is the devil. The Bible also says that angels are "... *ministering spirits sent forth to minister for those who will inherit salvation*"—Hebrews 1:14 (NKJV). The NIV Bible renders it that angels are "... *sent to serve those who will inherit salvation*." We are the heirs of salvation and angels serve us. If you read the book of Revelations, you will be amazed to see how incredibly powerful God's angels are.

We are also better armed. We have the invincible *Armor of God* that Apostle Paul mentioned in the book of Ephesians chapter 6:10–19. I discussed this later in the chapter "*Secrets of Great Strength*."

The Mind Is the Battlefield

Fear is a snare of the devil. The psalmist speaks of the "*snare of the fowler*"—Psalm 91:3. This is how it works. If the devil wants to cause death, sickness, barrenness, theft, accident, etc. to someone, he will first suggest a fear of that thing to the mind and heart of the person. It is the *devil's attack plan*. If the person accepts the fear and becomes afraid, he or she becomes susceptible to that fear happening which means that the person is caught in the snare.

This is because our mind is the battlefield. Apostle Paul talks of "*casting down imaginations*" and bringing into "*captivity every thought*"—2 Corinthians 10:5 (KJV). Imaginations and thoughts are processes of the mind. If you lose at the level of your mind, then, you have lost the battle.

What we often call "*The Temptation of Jesus*" is actually one of the clearest examples of spiritual warfare—and how to win it. We see the *combatants*: Jesus versus the devil, the Enemy. We see the *weapons*: Jesus wielding the Sword of the Spirit—the Word of God—against the devil's weapons of lies, deceit, and doubt. And we see the *battlefield*: it all took place in Jesus' mind.

The devil did not appear to Jesus physically; instead, he spoke directly to His mind. Our mind is the battlefield, and it is there that our victory or defeat is ultimately decided. This is where many people begin to lose the fight. Because they do not see a physical devil or demon nearby, they often assume that the thoughts the devil plants in their mind are their own.

According to the book of Luke chapter 4, Jesus was in the desert. Verse 5 says the devil led Jesus up to a high mountain and showed Him in an instant all the kingdoms of the world and their Glory. This could not possibly mean that Jesus was physically present on the mountain. No mountain, not even Mount Everest can afford anyone a view of all the kingdoms of the world. This would defy the laws of physics and will not be consistent with scientific principles regarding visibility, earth's curvature, and topography. Nevertheless, Jesus had this knowledge and visibility because He is the Creator of the world. This was in Jesus' mind, in His imagination.

In addition, in verse 9, it says that the devil brought Jesus to Jerusalem and had Him stand on the highest point of the temple. I do not know that it was even possible for anyone to stand on the pinnacle of the temple and I do not believe that Jesus left the wilderness to go to Jerusalem. Remember that the Bible says that He was led into the wilderness to be tempted (verses 1–2). Finally, Mark 1:13 says "... *He was there in the wilderness forty days, tempted by Satan.*" Therefore, Jesus was in the wilderness throughout. The temptations were all in the mind of our Lord and He won. If He did not win, He would have done the things the devil suggested.

To illustrate the point that you either win or lose in your mind, let me share with you two experiences that have two different outcomes:

While I was doing graduate studies, I lived on the fourth floor of my building or dormitory. One day, I was on the balcony of my room brushing my teeth, when this fear came that the glass cup I was holding would fall out of my hand. Not long after, the cup indeed fell from my hand and shattered because I did not rebuke or reject the thought.

Another time, while I was sitting down in the living room of my older brother, this fear came that the ceiling fan blowing above me would fall. The fear was sudden and strong. I knew it was the devil. There was no reason to warrant the fear. Therefore, I rebuke the spirit that sponsored the thought, rejected the thought and said that even if there is a reason for it to fall, that I uphold it by the word of God's power. The Bible says God upholds "... *all things by the word of his power*"—Hebrews 1:3 (NKJV). I believe that the fan would have fallen if I had not done anything. As soon as I rebuked the evil spirit behind the fear, as Jesus did, the fear left me.

I once heard a story of how a Christian preacher while driving home from a very successful preaching engagement, the devil told him that his car will veer off the road, that it will crash and that he will die in the crash. Immediately after while he was still rebuking the evil spirit behind the thought and was confessing the Word of God, his car indeed veered off the road and was heading for a ditch. Nevertheless, God intervened. You can imagine what would have happened if he had done nothing. It is that real.

The Devil's Weapons

Whenever the devil suggests a fear of death or sickness or anything negative to you, do not keep quiet, rebuke it. You may know and believe in your heart that " . . . *by His [Jesus] stripes we [you] have been healed"*—(Isaiah 53:5 NKJV) and that *"With long life I [God] will satisfy him [you] . . . "*—Psalms 91:16, say it to the devil. *The only way that the Word of God will work for you and that the devil will know that you know your covenant rights, is if you tell it to him boldly and loudly.*

At times, people experience a spiritual presence pressing down on them during sleep, triggering nightmares fueled by fear. If the concept of a spiritual entity weighing on someone in his or her sleep seems wild and outlandish, let me explain. In a semi-conscious, dreamlike state, you sense a presence atop you, pinning you down. You are aware of your surroundings, perhaps struggling to shake off this force, and though you may try to speak, no one hears you. If you have seen the widely acclaimed 2017 film *Get Out*, it is akin to the lead character's experience in the sunken place—fully aware, yet powerless, with his cries and words unheard.

The scientific explanation labels it "sleep paralysis," attributing it to neurological or psychological causes, but this is mistaken. Many cultures recognize this phenomenon by various names and understand it as a spiritual encounter. In North Atlantic folklore, it is known as "Old Hag" syndrome; in European traditions, it is called "Incubus" or "Succubus"; in Japan, it is "Kanashibari"; and in Middle Eastern lore, it is linked to "Jinn." I do not necessarily accept these cultural characterization but many African traditions, with their own names, like other cultures rightly identify it as a supernatural, demonic force at work.

Early in my Christian walk with the Lord when I was a young believer, the Lord taught me this through my own experiences. I found out that before I sleep, the devil would begin to give me thoughts and imaginations of fear. If I do not rebuke the thoughts, they just keep streaming, and if I were to sleep in that state, I would have nightmares and sometimes, a spiritual presence will press me down in my sleep.

If this is your experience, deal with your fears. Reject and cast out the thoughts and cast down the imaginations. Do not allow any fear to remain in your mind and heart before you sleep. You will discover that you will not have nightmares again and no spiritual presence will be able to press you down in your sleep.

These experiences may not all cease immediately but do not give up. As you continue to rebuke and resist, the fear will go away. You should know that " *. . . the Kingdom of Heaven has been forcefully advancing and violent people are attacking it*"—Matthew 11:12 (NLT).This verse means that there is real demonic opposition to God's kingdom and His people—believers. That is why, at times, you have to take hold of your inheritance by force, because there is an enemy who does not want you to have or enjoy it.

WEAPON OF LIES

Whatever you believe determines whether you win or lose in this war. Knowing the truth and believing it is crucial for winning your battles. Apostle Paul says in Ephesians Chapter 6:14 (NIV) "*Stand firm then, with the belt of truth buckled around your waist . . .*"

This verse tells me two things. First, the knowledge of the truth is important for our victory. If we do not know the truth or have believed a lie, the devil will use our lack of knowledge of the truth or our belief of a lie to either bring us into bondage or perpetuate his affliction or oppression of our lives.

Secondly, the fact that Paul listed the "*belt of truth*" first in the list of the components of the armor of God that he mentioned means that the knowledge of the truth is the number one weapon that you need in your spiritual arsenal.

This is understandable because the devil is, at his core, a liar. Jesus says that "*there is no truth in him*" and that "*he is a liar and the father of lies*"—John 8:44. Lying is natural to the devil because it is his "*native language.*" You must know that everything the devil tells you is a lie and that he is incapable of telling the truth.

You need to arm yourself with the knowledge of the truth to overcome the evil one. It is sometimes the case that after a preacher or minister or another believer has healed a person in the name of Jesus, the devil comes back to that person and tells him or her that they are not healed and they believe it. As a result, they remain sick and afflicted.

This is a lie because the Bible says "*And the prayer offered in faith will make the sick person well . . .*"—James 5:15 (NIV). If the person who prayed over you, prayed in faith and you believe the prayer, then, you are healed. It does not matter how you felt at the time. Feeling is not faith and it will come later. In addition, it does not matter what the devil says because Jesus says that Scripture cannot be broken—John 10:35. Neither your body nor the spirit of infirmity behind the sickness (if it has been caused by a demon) can disobey the Word of God.

Sometimes, the devil will tell you that the reason why the Lord will not heal you or that you are not healed is sin. This is a lie because James 5:15 says that the Lord will not only heal you, but "... *if he has sinned, he will be forgiven.*"

If your sickness is because of a sin or disobedience, the Bible says that the Lord will not only heal you but will also forgive you in response to your faith and your confession of that sin—verse 16. During His ministry, we saw Jesus healed many despite their sins. One notable example is the bedridden man at the pool of Bethesda who had been in the condition for 38 years—John 5:5. After Jesus healed him, He said to him "... *See, you have been made well. Sin no more, lest a worse thing come upon you.*" This indicates that the man's sickness was because of sin, yet Jesus healed him. If Jesus healed this man, you can be sure that He will heal you too.

Therefore, do not believe the lie of the devil. Do not even dwell on it because the devil may use it to introduce doubts into your heart. All you need to do is to tell the devil what the Word of God says and tell him to get away from you like Jesus told him when the devil tempted Him in Matthew 4.

Some other times, the devil would tell people that it is *not* God's will to heal them or that their sickness glorifies God. This is a lie because the Bible says "... *by his wounds you have been healed*"—1 Peter 2:24. If God wanted you to remain sick or your sickness or affliction glorifies God, Jesus will not have needed to receive those beatings.

Some ignorant people have used Jesus' statement in John 11:4 that Lazarus's sickness is "... *for the glory of God, that the Son of God may be glorified through it*" to justify their belief of the devil's lie that their sickness glorifies God. If Lazarus' sickness glorified God, Jesus would not have healed and brought him back to life. On the contrary, Jesus raising him back to life is what glorified God.

In addition, your sickness or affliction is not God ordained as some other people have inferred from John 9:3 where Jesus says concerning the man who was born blind: "'*Neither this man nor his parents sinned*' said Jesus, '*but this happened so that the work of God might be displayed in his life.*'" This does not mean that God ordained the man to be born blind so that God might be glorified, but that his blindness provided an opportunity for God to be glorified through Jesus displaying God's power by healing him.

God is never glorified by your affliction, nor is it God-ordained. God may use it for His own purpose as he did with Paul when he prayed that God should heal him. God said to him in 2 Corinthians 12:9 "*My grace is*

PART I. THE WEAPONS OF THE DEVIL'S WARFARE

sufficient for you, for my power is made perfect in your weakness . . . " However, he never ordained it. In fact, Paul said that his affliction was the work of a *"messenger of Satan"*—verse 7; it was never God's doing.

You must never accept the lie that God wants you to have or live with any sickness, disease, medical condition, whatever they may be: ulcer, migraine, asthma, malaria, barrenness or be oppressed in your sleep or dream or that He does not want to heal or deliver you from them. The salvation of God is a total package; it includes our healing. The Bible says that the stripes of Jesus heals us. This means that healing is included in our salvation and redemption.

Apostle John, speaking by the Holy Spirit says, *"Beloved, I pray that you may prosper in all things and be in health, just as your soul prospers"*—3 John 2 (NKJV). It is God heart's desire that you should prosper and have sound and holistic health. Amen. Stop believing the devil's lie.

When I was a teenager and a new believer in the Lord Jesus, I was suffering from demonic oppression. The devil told me that I was possessed by a demon, and I believed it. This did three things to me: One, it produced in me the belief that I was a captive; two, that I cannot deliver myself and therefore helpless; three, that I needed deliverance.

I heard of a Christian brother who has been a believer for a long time and was in fact, a minister, but he was always asking for spiritual deliverance. The only reason he would be doing this is that this brother has believed the lie that he is possessed.

I was in this situation for some time until the Lord showed me through the Bible—His Word that I was not possessed and taught me how to overcome the oppression. I am aware that some Christian ministers are still teaching that a Christian can be possessed. However, I want you to know that it is a lie from the depths of Hell. I believe and say this based on the authority of the Word of God.

The Bible says—if you are born again and filled with the Holy Spirit—that " *. . . do you not know that your body is the temple of the Holy Spirit who is in you, whom you have from God, and you are not your own?"*—1 Corinthians 6:19. This means that, if you are a Christian filled with the Holy Spirit, you cannot be possessed. If your body is a temple of the Holy Spirit, (and of course, a spirit cannot inhabit another spirit), and you are God's possession, then it is not possible for you to be possessed by another spirit.

On the authority of God's Word, I say that you cannot be possessed because there is no fellowship between righteousness and unrighteousness, and there is no communion between light and darkness—2 Corinthians 6:14. The Holy Spirit will not dwell in your body in partnership with a demon.

The Holy Spirit must have left for a demon to come in. In John 13:27, after Jesus gave Judas a piece of bread at the last supper, the Bible says " . . . *Satan entered him.*" So, even Judas did not become possessed by the devil until the very last moment after Jesus gave him up. Except God has given you up, the devil cannot possess you because you are God's possession. This was also the same in the Old Testament story of King Saul. After Samuel, the Prophet anointed Saul king, he told him in 1 Samuel 10:5-7 that he will be filled with the Spirit of the Lord when he enters the city and meets a procession of prophets. He was and even prophesied.

The Spirit of God remained on King Saul until after he had repeatedly disobeyed the Lord. The Bible says in 1 Samuel 16:14 that "*Now the Spirit of the Lord had departed from Saul, and an evil spirit from the Lord tormented him.*" An evil spirit possessed him only after the Spirit of God had left him. The evidence of his possession was that he attempted to kill David twice with his spear and made a series of other bad decisions.

A sure indication that God has not given you up is the continued presence of the Holy Spirit in your life. It is not recorded anywhere in the book of Acts that a born again Christian was ever delivered of demon possession. Scripture does not support this teaching that a Christian can be possessed by a demon, so it is a lie. The Word of God is the Truth, the Only Truth and the Whole Truth. Therefore, any knowledge or teaching, no matter how convincing it may be or whoever may have taught it, if it does not line up with the Word of God, is a Lie, pure and simple.

You need to know this, which is why you must give yourself to the study of the Word. It is your sure defense against the lies of the devil. The devil has no right to afflict you. God has not given him that right. As a child of God, the Bible says that God has delivered you from the dominion of darkness—Colossians 1:13. The devil and his cohorts have no authority or power over you. The son of God has set you free and you are free indeed—John 8:36. Do not believe the devil's lie.

If the devil tells you that you're going to be barren because there has been a history of barrenness in your family, tell him that you are a new creation—2 Corinthians 5:17—and that the Scripture says " . . . *none will miscarry or be barren in your land*"—Exodus 23:26. It is your inheritance because you are a child of God.

If the devil tells you that you will die early because there has been a history of early male or female deaths in your family, tell him that God has said he will satisfy you with long life—Psalm 91:16.

Perhaps the lie that the devil has told you is that God has not forgiven you or that you are guilty of something that you are, in fact, not guilty of before God. Remember that the Bible says, *"If our hearts condemn us, we know that God is greater than our hearts, and he knows everything"*—1 John 3:20. Apostle John is saying that our hearts may condemn us for something God does not condemn. Making believers feel guilty for something that God does not condemn is a tactic of the devil. If you feel guilty over something and you do not understand why, learn what the Word of God says about it and if the Bible does not condemn it, then your guilt is from the devil. Reject it.

Conversely, we may also feel justified in doing something that God condemns. This is why I am skeptical when someone says *"my heart told me to do it"* or I recoil when I hear *"go with your gut"* or *"do what makes you happy."* The Bible is our guide, not your heart. If what your heart is telling you to do does not line up with the Word of God, you must know that your heart is wrong no matter how convinced you may be. It is like a believer believing that it is okay to marry an unbeliever. It is not okay because the Bible says it is not.

God does speak to our hearts or minds but so does the devil. This is why you must judge everything by the Word of God. In fact, the Bible says, *"The heart is deceitful above all things, And desperately wicked . . . "*—Jeremiah 17:9. In Genesis, when God expressed His regret at creating humans, the Bible says that God saw *" . . . that every intent of the thoughts of his heart was only evil continually"*—Genesis 6:5. God can guide us through our hearts but our heart is not a reliable guide. The Word of God is our 100% reliable guide.

Mental Health

Mental health issues are now considered a public health crisis due to its pervasiveness. In media and entertainment, we have seen people commit suicide. We have seen it in sports with athletes who commit suicide, withdraw from competitions or can no longer play effectively. We have seen it in every sphere of industry, in politics, in healthcare among doctors and nurses, in the legal profession and emergency services and in everyday life.

We treat it as a medical and/or psychological condition with medicine and counseling which is appropriate in most cases. For those who are not born again believers, this is their only option. In other cases though, treating it with medications or therapy is merely superficial because it is treating symptoms and not the underlying causes.

I want to say this in as loving a manner as possible, as a believer, you must know that while not every mental health issue may be mental illness, a significant portion is. Where there is thoughts of suicide, of self-harm or of doing harm to others, or persistent depression or prolonged anxiety, it is mental illness and it is rooted in demonic oppression. Any of these conditions is caused by demons and is a spiritual illness. Only the power of God can cure spiritual illness. Medicine or therapy may help in some cases but in chronic cases, patients take medications long term or for the rest of their lives without ever being healed.

Doctors and psychotherapists want us to believe that only genetics, biology and our environments can explain all medical or mental conditions. However, as a believer you must understand that there is a spiritual dimension to life and the solutions to some of life's problems can be found only in the spiritual.

Oftentimes, it is demons that cause physical and mental illnesses. We see this many times in the ministry of Jesus. For example, a demon was responsible for the condition of the epileptic (physical illness) boy in Matthew chapter 17 whose father begged Jesus to heal. Jesus healed the boy by casting out the demon. The maniac in Mark chapter 5 who had lost control of his mind (mental illness), lived among the tombs and could not be bound or restrained by anyone had a spiritual condition. He isolated himself and had no human contact or relationship because demons possessed his body. As soon as Jesus cast out those demons, his mind was restored. When the townspeople came to see him, the Bible says he was dressed and in his *"right mind."* His was an extreme case of demonic possession but he was not in his right mind before because of this possession.

When we see people behave in ways that are not rational or normal, they have acute or unexplained anxieties, or they have extreme and uncontrolled mood swings, we say it is a mental health issue. However, whenever any of these behaviors or conditions are prolonged and resistant to any treatment or counseling it is demonic oppression of the mind. King Saul in the Bible is one person that exhibited evidence of mental illness. After the Spirit of God left him, 1 Samuel 16:14 says, an evil spirit tormented him.

Subsequently, he began to harbor homicidal thoughts toward David—and even toward his own son Jonathan—and on multiple occasions, he hurled his spear in an attempt to kill them. This was all due to the evil spirit that preyed on his mind.

Transgender ideology where biological males transition to females or vice versa, gender dysphoria where people say that they are uncomfortable with the gender they are born with, gender fluidity where individuals identify as neither male nor female, often using pronouns like "they or them" (non-binary), or embracing a range of gender identities that may shift over time are mental illnesses. These are all disorders of the mind caused by demonic oppression.

When we see people experience or display these kinds of mental illness behaviors, as believers, we must show understanding and deal with them with compassion and not hostility regardless of our political leaning or belief system because they are demonic oppression.

Mental illness or demonic oppression can result from demons preying on the minds of their targets. Over time, if the person does not recognize what is happening, does not know how to respond, or lacks the power to resist, they begin to accept the suggested thoughts as their own.

I believe that the way Jesus responded to Peter in Matthew 16:21–23 KJV is a model for us on how to respond to any negative thoughts that are contrary to the Word of God concerning us. When Peter objected to Jesus dying on the cross, Jesus recognized that it was the devil speaking through Peter and so He rebuked the devil speaking through Peter at that time. He said " . . . *Get behind Me, Satan! You are an offense to Me, for you are not mindful of the things of God, but the things of men.*" Jesus was not saying that Peter was the devil but He knew that Peter, even though he meant well, was not speaking by the Holy Spirit at that time. We must learn to recognize and respond when the devil puts a thought or idea in our minds or speaks them to us even if it is through a loved one like Peter. Jesus did not ignore what Peter said, you must also not ignore any thought that the devil plants in your mind. You must reject it.

None of us is impervious to these demonic suggestions. We must reject them on the authority of the Word of God and rebuke the spirit behind them. As believers, we must never allow evil thoughts to grow in our minds and lives.

The Devil's Weapons

WEAPON OF IGNORANCE

Knowledge is power. The Bible says, *"A wise man is strong, Yes, a man of knowledge increases strength;."*—Proverbs 24:5 (NKJV). If you are ignorant of how the devil operates, it will be difficult for you to keep yourself free from demonic control and oppression.

Galatians 5:1 (NKJV) declares, *"Stand fast therefore in the liberty by which Christ has made us free, and do not be entangled again with a yoke of bondage."* You must understand it is your duty to stand fast or firm in this liberty or freedom. If you do not hold your ground, you risk falling back into the chains of bondage. One key way to stand fast is to recognize the devil's schemes and know how to counter his tactics.

Because many are ignorant, they return or remain under the yoke of bondage. Jesus says " . . . *you will know the truth and the truth will set you free"*—John 8:32. No matter how strong a yoke is, whenever a person grasps the relevant truth, he or she can break the yoke.

In Isaiah 10:27 (NIV), Prophet Isaiah declares, " . . . *the yoke will be broken because you have grown so fat."* The imagery depicts a farmer placing a yoke on animals, like bulls or horses, to control and utilize them. When an animal grows too fat for the yoke, the farmer must remove it to prevent the animal's death. Similarly, when a believer, once bound by the devil's yoke, grows spiritually fat, the yoke breaks, and the devil loses control.

The more you know God's truth, the stronger you grow fat with His anointing, breaking every yoke of bondage. I stand by this based on Scripture and my own life experiences, where I have seen it work.

Often, or perhaps frequently, God's people go from one church meeting to another or from one Christian leader to another, seeking deliverance or healing, when what they truly need is specific revelation or knowledge. They may fast repeatedly and pray fervently, but without this knowledge, nothing will change.

It is often observed that some individuals, even after receiving prayer for deliverance or healing, experience freedom only briefly before falling back into bondage. Why does this happen? The reason lies in a lack of knowledge to sustain that freedom. Jesus has indeed set us free, but many believers fail to maintain it due to insufficient understanding of how to appropriate and uphold their victory. The devil exploits this ignorance, gaining an advantage over those unaware of his schemes.

In the account of the fall in the Garden of Eden, recorded in Genesis chapter 3, we see how the devil took advantage of Eve's ignorance to deceive her. His strategy was to first sow doubt in Eve's mind by using a strawman argument. He distorts God's clear and generous command as restrictive and arbitrary. God told Adam and Eve they could eat from any tree in the garden, except the tree of the knowledge of good and evil. When that failed, the devil prompted her to question the wisdom of God's command paving the way for the deception and lie that they would not die but would instead become like God.

Let me illustrate the conversation the devil had with Eve by adapting it to one of the most consequential and so-called "controversial" issues of our time: fornication—premarital sex or sex outside of marriage. It is considered controversial only from the world's perspective, but God's Word is clear that it is sin.

>Devil: "Did God really say to not have sex?"
>Human: "No, he only says to not have sex outside of marriage"
>Devil: "Sex is a natural emotion and God gave you the emotion so how can it be wrong?"
>Human: "I wonder why God would keep me from doing something that He gave me"

Then comes the coup de grace, the trick, the lie.

>Devil: "God wants you to be happy.
>Having sex makes you happy.
>So, it is okay to do what makes you happy."

The devil begins by distorting God's command about sex, as he did with Eve, to stir doubt. The human, like Eve, responds with certainty about God's clear directive. When that fails, the devil argues that sex, a God-given biological desire, cannot be wrong—and the human starts to buy it. As doubt takes root, he introduces the lie that it is all about personal happiness. This mirrors how Eve was deceived into thinking she would not die but would become like God. Does not that tactic sound all too familiar?

The Sun Tzu quote that I previously referenced is actually part of a larger quote that is as follows:

>*If you know the enemy and know yourself,*
>*you need not fear the result of a hundred battles.*
>*If you know yourself but not the enemy,*
>*for every victory gained you will also suffer a defeat.*
>*If you know neither the enemy nor yourself,*
>*you will succumb in every battle.*

The Devil's Weapons

The Art of War

This quote underscores the vital importance of understanding both your enemy and yourself in spiritual warfare. You must be aware of the demonic forces working against you and recognize the devil's strategies and schemes. Without this understanding, you are at risk of defeat. Equally important is knowing who you are in the Lord and the provisions He has made for your victory—without that, you remain vulnerable.

Knowing yourself also involves being honest about your moral weaknesses. Do not put yourself in situations where you know you are likely to fall. Samson had a known weakness for women, so spending time with someone like Delilah—who ultimately led to his downfall—was unwise and dangerous. Paul told the Thessalonians, *"Abstain from all appearance of evil."* (1 Thessalonians 5:22) and Timothy, *"Flee also youthful lusts . . . ."* Joseph avoided being alone with Potiphar's wife because he recognized that she had intentions toward him that were sexual in nature. The Bible says that Joseph not only refused to sleep with her, but he would not " . . . *even be with her*" (Genesis 39:10, NIV).

Proverbs 1:10–19 urges us to avoid the company of those who try to lure or tempt us into doing wrong. It warns that choosing the wrong path may seem rewarding at first, but it always leads to destruction. Though such people may appear to succeed for a time, in the end, they are caught in the very traps their actions have set.

If your struggle is with alcohol, avoid spending time in bars or maintaining friendships and relationships where you might be pressured or influenced to drink. Victory in spiritual warfare requires more than just awareness of the enemy—it also demands self-awareness and the discipline to make wise, intentional choices.

In the next chapter, I will discuss how to recognize your enemy in conflict situations and I will explore the spiritual dimensions of life and conflicts.

PART II

KNOW YOUR ENEMY

Chapter 4

Recognize the Enemy

Out of the mouth of babes and sucklings hast thou ordained strength because of thine enemies, that thou mightest still the enemy and the avenger.
Psalms 8:2 (KJV)

AN UNDERSTANDING OF WHO our enemy is the first step to winning the battles of life. We cannot fight and win if we are fighting the wrong person. If you are ignorant of whom your enemy is, you may be fighting the wrong person. That many are ignorant of who their real enemy is, is evident.

When your colleague in the workplace is scheming to have you removed from your position or fired, or your boss, because you refuse to go along with an unethical request or to violate a company policy, is making your work life unpleasant, whom do you fight? As a student, do you regard your supervisor or teacher who is just impossible as your enemy? Do you take your difficult and hard to please husband or wife to be your enemy? When your neighbor is hostile to you, with or without cause, or somebody insults, slanders or lies against you, can you recognize who the enemy is?

The list is endless. In addition, we must admit that we often fight the human agents instead. *Every opposition or hostility against you in the physical, through whatever person, is merely a manifestation of the spiritual.* Therefore, if you fight the human agent, then, as Paul told the Corinthians " . . . *you have been completely defeated already.*"—1 Corinthians 6:7 (NIV).

Paul spoke out because the Corinthian believers were suing each other in court over their disputes. Instead of battling the spiritual forces stirring up their disagreements and conflicts, they attacked one another. If you are doing the same, you have already lost the fight before it begins.

Sometimes, we see churches and believers caught in deep division and bitterness. Christians break into groups, turning on each other with hostility. Rather than uniting to face the true enemy, they waste energy fighting among themselves, while the devil stands back, mocking their chaos.

These examples reveal that many do not recognize the true enemy. When you repay evil with evil, matching wrong for wrong or offense for offense, you have let evil defeat you, as Romans 12:21 warns against.

OUR COMMON ENEMY

There is one basic enemy and our common enemy. Our text, Psalm 8: 2 says *"thine enemies"* and *"the enemy."* The enemies are the hosts of darkness. Paul says we wrestle *"against principalities, against powers, against the rulers of the darkness of this world, against spiritual wickedness in high places"*— KJV. Alternatively, as the NIV translates it " . . . *spiritual forces of evil in the Heavenly realms."* Ephesians 6:12.

The devil is *"the enemy."* Apostle Peter says in 1 Peter 5:8, *"Be alert and of sober mind. Your enemy the devil prowls around like a roaring lion looking for someone to devour."* The devil is the real enemy and the source of all enmity. The *"enemies"* are the collective hosts of darkness who are loyal to the devil. They are the fallen Angels that *"kept not their first estate"* (KJV) or did not *"keep their positions of authority"* (NIV) Jude 6.

Our true enemies are not our in-laws, spouse, uncle, coworker, or boss. This does not mean human enemies do not exist—they do, but they are just tools. Some are deliberate agents, while most are unaware pawns. If we treat them as the real enemy, we have already lost the fight.

SPIRITUAL DIMENSION TO CONFLICT

In the Sermon on the Mount, Jesus laid out new lines of truth. At times, He corrected wrong interpretations of Old Testament laws that had built up over the years; other times, He updated those laws. Jesus had the right to do this because, first, He is the Truth, as He declared, *"I am the Way, the Truth, and the Life"* (John 14:6). No truth surpasses or compares to what Jesus says. Second, Jesus is the fullness of divine revelation. Hebrews 1:1–2 says

Recognize the Enemy

In the past God spoke to our ancestors through the prophets
at many times and in various ways,
but in these last days he has spoken to us by his Son
(NIV)

Since Jesus' death and resurrection, we have been in "the last days." Jesus is God's final voice to humanity, with no new revelation to come. As teachers, preachers, and believers, we only repeat what Jesus has already spoken. He is the Son of God, God's ultimate and last word to us, not the false prophets or self-proclaimed messengers of other faiths.

Some Old Testament laws were concessions Moses allowed for the Israelites. For instance, Matthew 5:31 and Deuteronomy 24:1 permit a man to divorce his wife by giving her a certificate of divorce. Jesus later explains in Matthew 19:7–8 that this was not God's original plan; Moses only allowed it because of their stubborn hearts.

In Matthew 5:38, Jesus said, "*You've heard it was said, 'an eye for an eye, and a tooth for a tooth.'*" He was about to update or correct—depending on your view—an old law or tradition. That Old Testament rule allowed people to repay a wrong with an equal wrong, like "*eye for eye.*" "*Eye for eye and tooth for tooth" refers to physical retribution—it symbolizes a response through physical action.* Back then, most people did not grasp the spiritual side of conflicts. Only a few, like Moses, Joshua, David, Elijah, and Elisha, had some insight into this. Wars were fought mostly based on the recognition of human enemies, not the spiritual forces behind them.

Let me digress a bit to share this. It might surprise some of you, but God does approve of certain wars—not all wars are wrong. For example, God ordered Joshua to fight battles to take the land of Canaan. He also told Saul to wage war against the Amalekites for their attacks on Israel in Exodus 17. These were righteous wars required by God. One of God's names, *Jehovah Sabaoth*, means "The Lord of Hosts," where "hosts" refers to Heaven's armies. This shows God as the Commander of Heaven's forces. In Revelation 19:11–16, we see Jesus leading these heavenly armies as their mighty King.

However, let me be very clear that most wars that humanity has fought in the history of the world are not righteous. In fact, righteous wars are rare and most wars are just hegemonic wars of conquest, of exploitation, of genocide, and of colonialism. These are not righteous wars at all but are wars inspired by demonic forces.

PART II. KNOW YOUR ENEMY

Getting back to the topic of *'eye for eye'*, and *'tooth for tooth'*. I do not believe that God wants us to use violence against those we consider our enemies or form militant groups to battle them. I am aware that there are communities where Christian believers have advocated the principle of an *eye for eye* and a *tooth for tooth*. Some of these belief systems grew out of historical, racial or religious injustices. For example, in American communities where people have been the target of racial violence or in the northern part of my native country where Christian minorities have often been the targets of violent Muslim jihadists. However, you must understand that Jesus has changed the laws because He went ahead to add in verses 39–41 that

> *But I tell you, do not resist an evil person.*
> *If anyone slaps you on the right cheek, turn to them the other cheek also.*
> *And if anyone wants to sue you and take your shirt, hand over your coat as well.*
> *If anyone forces you to go one mile, go with them two miles.*
> (NIV)

He began by saying *"But I tell you . . . "* signaling that He wants us to do things differently. Then He said, " . . . *do not resist an evil person."* This is Jesus updating the law. He modeled for us how not to use violence against our human enemies throughout His ministry, arrest and torture. For example, in the Garden of Gethsemane, He admonished Peter for cutting off the right ear of the servant of the High Priest—John 18:11.

However, while I understand that He does not want us to resort to physical retribution or violence, I initially did not understand nor could accept Him saying " . . . *do not resist an evil person."* I wondered if He meant that if someone points a gun at me or comes at me with a sword, I should do nothing to defend myself. I wondered if he meant that I should do nothing against my attacker, even though I may be able to disarm him or her or run away.

I kept contemplating this until the Holy Spirit gave me understanding. It would be foolish for me, or any of us to do nothing if we could. However, in saying that, I believe that Jesus was revealing a truth that was not yet known or understood. Jesus was drawing attention to the fact that the human person was not the real enemy.

This becomes very clear when you understand the historical context. It was at a time of Roman occupation of Judea, which was often harsh and oppressive for Jews. Roman soldiers commonly confiscated possessions or forced locals to carry their military equipment during travels, as exemplified by Simon of Cyrene, who was compelled to carry Jesus' cross in Mark 15:21.

Roman oppression in Judea fueled Jewish resentment and resistance. In this context, the Zealots, a militant group advocating armed rebellion, gained prominence. One of Jesus' disciples, Simon the Zealot (Matthew 10:4), was likely associated with such zealous views before following Jesus.

When Jesus said, "*do not resist an evil person*," He wanted to shift our focus from the physical to the spiritual. He wanted us to recognize the *evil* behind the person. The devil is the evil one. In Matthew 6:13, Jesus taught that we should pray that God would deliver us from the evil one. Therefore, He was saying, "*Do not fight the human agents but fight the devils behind them.*"

Human beings are not the real enemies but the demons behind who are instigating and manipulating them. It is these spiritual powers we should resist, not the human vessels. For the Jews, they were not to resist their human Roman overloads but the demonic oppressors behind them. If you understand it this way, then what He says in verses 39–41, that we should *turn the other cheek, hand over our coat,* or *go the extra mile,* becomes understandable.

I once read a book by a pastor who offered an interesting explanation of verses 39–41. He said that Jesus is not instructing us to let ourselves be cheated. Instead, if we love our enemy who strikes us on one cheek, they will be unable to strike again, even if we turn the other cheek. By responding with grace and forgiveness, they are less likely to harm us further. Why? Because by loving them, we disarm their hostility.

Similarly, if you deal with the enemy behind your human enemy, you disarm him or her. Having struck you on one cheek, they cannot strike you again because by subduing the demon that is at work through them, you prevail over them.

I also believe that Jesus is saying that we should do all that we can to deescalate conflicts. Oftentimes, people get hurt unnecessarily because they do not know how to do this. When facing, for example, someone with a gun or someone who is physically stronger, the last thing you should do is provoke them with words and escalate the tension. In Matthew 10:16, Jesus said, "*. . . be wise as serpents . . .* " This is a fitting analogy, as snakes are generally cautious animals that avoid unnecessary encounters. For example, the rattlesnake will often rattle its tail as a warning signal—a final attempt to prevent conflict.

Jesus showed us the way in this. He often avoided conflicts or walked away from dangerous situations. In John chapter 10, because Jesus claimed to be the Son of God, the Jews got upset and *"Therefore they sought again to seize Him, but He escaped out of their hand"*—verse 39. Then He traveled beyond the Jordan, where He was when He heard Lazarus had died. When He told His disciples He was returning, they were puzzled, asking why He would go back since the Jews had earlier tried to stone Him—John 11:8.

There is a story in Luke 4:24–30 where Jesus rebukes the people of Nazareth for their unbelief by contrasting it with the faith of the widow of Zarephath and Naaman the Syrian—both non-Jews. The crowd did not take it well. In verse 29, they led Him to the edge of a hill, planning to throw Him off. However, in verse 30, the Bible says, " . . . *passing through the midst of them, He went His way.*" Do you think that happened by chance? Not at all. This is what victory in spiritual warfare looks like.

Jesus fully understood the spiritual realities behind daily life and conflict, and He knew how to engage the spiritual enemy. He often prayed in private, and I believe some of those prayers were aimed at confronting the spiritual forces He would face each day. This is the same mindset we must have if we are to prevail in our own battles. Remember, Jesus taught us to pray, " . . . *deliver us from the evil one . . .* " (Matthew 6:13). He also said, " . . . *Each day's own evil is sufficient.*" (Matthew 6:34 WEB). Each day carries its own evil that we must guard against—this is why we must pray daily.

Beyond avoiding or defusing conflict, you must also recognize and disarm the demonic forces working behind your enemies. Jesus understood this clearly—that is why He returned across the Jordan without fear, even though His disciples were concerned. You can do the same by invoking the name of Jesus or by praying in tongues. However, understand this: you must be a born-again believer to invoke the name of Jesus. It would not work for just anyone. Remember the sons of Sceva in Acts 19:13–16—they had no relationship with Jesus, and when they tried to use His name, it backfired.

I will say more about speaking or praying in tongues later, but for now, here is a story of God's power being released through speaking in tongues. One midnight, I was walking home from a prayer meeting through a quiet, familiar neighborhood I often passed through during the day. Out of nowhere, three dogs resembling Great Danes charged at me suddenly. Instinctively, I shouted at them, speaking in tongues. The moment I did, they fled and vanished as mysteriously as they appeared. I looked around but could not find them or figure out where they went. Frankly, it seems they were not of this world.

Speaking or praying in tongues is a very powerful thing to do when faced with a situation where you do not know what to do or pray. I discussed praying in tongues in more detail in chapter nine.

Joseph the Dreamer

The story of Joseph and the plot against him vividly illustrates the spiritual dimensions of life and conflict, revealing the hidden motives, machinations, and maneuvers of the key figures involved. It offers a behind-the-scenes view of both the visible and the invisible actors—the divine and the demonic. In this story, we see the *devil's attack plan* laid out which we need to learn to recognize and counter.

In Genesis 37, we read that Jacob loved Joseph more than he loved his other sons because Joseph was born to him in his old age. This favoritism, combined with Joseph's dreams of one day ruling over his brothers, fueled their hatred for him. One day, Jacob sent Joseph to check on his brothers, who were tending their flocks, and to bring them provisions. When they saw him approaching from a distance, they plotted to kill him, saying,

> *Look, this dreamer is coming! Come therefore, let us now kill him and cast him into some pit; and we shall say, 'Some wild beast has devoured him.' We shall see what will become of his dreams!*
> (NKJV)

This was the *devil's attack plan*. He instigated Joseph's brothers to kill him, specifically to prevent his dream from coming true. Do you think this was their own idea? It may seem so, but it was not. The devil exploited their hatred and jealousy, planting the idea and thoughts in their minds.

God intervened by using Reuben to persuade the brothers not to kill Joseph. The devil then planted the idea in Judah's mind to sell him instead. Reasoning that if he could not get the brothers to kill Joseph, he aimed to condemn him to a life of slavery, believing a slave could never become a ruler or governor. However, God responded again, orchestrating events so the Midianites sold Joseph to Potiphar in Egypt—the very place where God would fulfill Joseph's dreams. Satan was unaware of this, and God outmaneuvered him. God will always counter the devil's moves as long as you align your life, goals, and ambitions with His plan for you. Hallelujah!

You might wonder why the devil did not target Joseph's brothers or why they did not experience the same level of demonic hostility that he did. The reason is clear, and it is still relevant today. The devil suspected that God had a special plan for Joseph, though he did not know exactly what or how. Similarly, if you are facing demonic opposition—perhaps without even realizing it—it may indicate that God has a special purpose for your life. Be assured that God will outmaneuver Satan on your behalf.

Thirteen years later, when they met Joseph again, his brothers deeply regretted their actions. They likely wondered how they could have considered killing their own brother. While their regret does not absolve their guilt, it is important to recognize that demonic forces were at play. Joseph understood this, which made it easier for him to forgive them. He told them that God had sent him ahead to save their lives through a great deliverance (Genesis 45:7).

In society, we see parents killing their own children and vice-versa, siblings murdering each other as Cain killed Abel, and friends betraying friends with deadly outcomes. These acts are unnatural and stem from demonic thoughts planted by the devil. Yet, the perpetrators often carry them out, believing these ideas are their own. We must be vigilant and quick to reject every ungodly or evil thought that enters our minds.

Paul says, *"For though we walk in the flesh, we do not war after the flesh."*—2 Corinthians 10:3 (KJV). In addition, *" . . . we wrestle not against flesh and blood . . . "* Ephesians 6:12 (KJV). Human beings are just agents and are not our real enemies. The devil and his demonic hosts are our real enemies and are the ones that we must fight. If you know this, then you have taken the first step to becoming an overcomer.

GOD'S ENEMIES

Going back to our main text in Psalm 8:2. I want you to note two things:

First, it says *"thine enemies."* Remember, King David, the psalmist, was speaking to God. When he said *"thine enemies,"* he meant God's enemies. This shows your enemies are also God's enemies. Therefore, take heart—this means anyone opposing you is battling God Himself. Your foes are God's foes too. In truth, they are mainly His enemies. Those who hate you really hate God.

Therefore, you are not alone in fighting against them; God himself is also fighting against them. He has promised, *" . . . I will be an enemy to your enemies and an adversary to your adversaries"*—Exodus 23:22. In addition, He will " . . . *make your enemies a footstool for your feet"*—Psalms 110:1.

David understood that the enemies of God's people are God's enemies. That is why he told Goliath " . . . *for the battle is the Lord's, and he will give all of you into our hands."*—1 Samuel 17:47. The Lord will also deliver your enemies into your hands. Amen. In 2 chronicles 20:15 (NIV), the prophet told Jehoshaphat and the people " . . . *This is what the Lord says to you: Do not be afraid or discouraged because of this vast army for the battle is not yours but God's."*

The Lord has never lost a battle, can never lose any, and will not lose yours. You should therefore be encouraged. The battles of your life are God's, He will win, and you will win. Amen.

Second, notice that the Scripture says God has ordained strength to " . . . *still the enemy and the avenger."* Although it mentions *"thine enemies,"* it does not say to still the enemies but *the enemy*. This points to the devil as the true enemy. By silencing him, you silence all enemies—human or spiritual. The Bible promises, " . . . *resist the devil, and he will flee from you"* (James 4:7). You may not always be able to recognize your human or spiritual foes, but if you resist and overcome the devil, you defeat them too. You can subdue the devil—God's Word guarantees it.

Silencing the enemy is the next vital step to prevailing in spiritual warfare. I will explore this further in the next chapter.

Chapter 5

Silence the Enemy and Avenger

Out of the mouth of babes and sucklings hast thou ordained strength because of thine enemies, that thou mightest still the enemy and the avenger.
Psalms 8:2 (KJV)

I HAVE NOTICED A trend in the church where some believers rely on others to fight their spiritual battles. When they are sick, they immediately seek someone else to pray for them. While the Bible instructs us to call for the elders of the church when we are sick (James 5:14), you should also learn to pray for yourself and trust God for your healing, unless you have already tried and still have not received healing.

When these believers face troubles at home, they quickly turn to another believer to pray and fast on their behalf. When nightmares or dream attacks occur, they hurriedly seek someone else's help. If someone threatens or opposes them at work, in their neighborhood, or at school, they panic and run to another Christian for prayers. It is akin to how nations sometimes hire mercenaries (soldiers of fortune) to fight their battles for them.

If you live like this, you will never grow your faith and you will never learn how to win. I believe that no minister, brother, or sister should ever encourage a fellow believer to live like that. I do know that the Bible says *"two are better than one . . . "* and that *"though one may be overpowered, two can defend themselves. A cord of three strands is not quickly broken."* Ecclesiastes 4:9 & 12. In fact, you may need others to join with you to win some battles, which is why you cannot have the mentality of a lone ranger.

This was one of the mistakes of Samson. We need to bear one another burden—Galatians 6:2.

You must understand that your battles are primarily your own. If you seek prayers, ask someone to pray with you, not to take over your prayers entirely. Avoid developing a habit of handing your battles to others to fight on your behalf. Know that there are no mercenaries in the kingdom of God; every believer is a soldier and an active combatant in God's army.

GOD IS ON YOUR SIDE

Always remember that your enemies are also God's enemies. Anyone who stands against you is standing against God Himself, and no one can fight God and win. You never face your battles alone. Jehovah Shammah—the Lord who is always present—is with you every step of the way. Let your faith be anchored in this truth, not in any minister or so-called "prayer warrior." The Bible says:

> *God is our refuge and strength,*
> *an ever-present help in trouble.*
> *Therefore we will not fear, though the Earth give way*
> *and the mountains fall into the heart of the sea.*
> Psalms 46:1–2 (NIV)

Martin Luther, the great reformer, penned "A Mighty Fortress Is Our God." God is our impregnable Fortress, a strong tower of strength. Place your trust in this truth as you face your battles.

THE GOOD FIGHT OF FAITH

In 1 Timothy 6:12, Paul writes to Timothy, *"Fight the good fight of faith"* (NKJV). Notice Paul does not tell Timothy to find someone else to battle for him—he says Timothy must fight himself. In addition, Paul makes it clear it is a fight, even if it is a good one. Let me explain why this fight is worth fighting.

It is a good fight because the outcome is already settled and decided in your favor. You are not battling to win—you are fighting to claim the victory Jesus has already secured for you.

That is why you are called *"more than a conqueror"* in Romans 8:37 (NKJV). A conqueror fights to win, but a more-than-conqueror steps into battle knowing the victory is already won. If you do not grasp this, the devil will keep overpowering you. You're not fighting to maybe win—you're fighting to claim and enforce the victory Jesus has already given you, taking hold of what is rightfully yours.

That is why Paul urges us to fight in 1 Timothy 6:12. You have to battle to claim what belongs to you. Without fighting, the victory stays unrealized in your life. You cannot call someone a conqueror unless they have faced a war, an overcomer unless they have fought a battle, or a winner unless they have entered a contest.

Scripture tells us that Jesus " . . . *disarmed principalities and powers, making a public spectacle of them, triumphing over them*" (Colossians 2:15, NKJV). Though Jesus has already defeated the devil for us, that victory only becomes ours when we fight to claim it. You have to battle to take hold of what is yours.

Many Christians struggle to understand why they do not experience divine healing, even though Scripture says they're healed by Jesus' stripes (1 Peter 2:24). They wonder why oppression lingers, despite God's promise in Isaiah 54:14 (KJV), "*In righteousness shalt thou be established: thou shalt be far from oppression.*"

The reason is that they are ignorant of the fact that it is their responsibility to silence the enemy in their lives. Jesus says, " . . . *the kingdom of heaven suffers violence, and the violent take it by force*"—Matthew 11:12 (NKJV). This means that demonic forces constantly oppose the kingdom of God—the Church. The devil is the enemy who does not want you to enjoy your covenant rights and blessings. You must take it by force.

> *And from the days of John the Baptist until now*
> *the kingdom of heaven suffers violence,*
> *and the violent take it by force.*

The devil will not always let you claim your Kingdom blessings without a struggle—you have got to take them by force. You must fight to make divine healing and God's other promises yours. I had to battle to secure divine healing and many other blessings for myself.

You have to fight the battle yourself, but God's forces will stand with you. In Judges 5:19–23, the Lord's angels were there, fighting alongside Israel against Sisera's army. The Bible says in verses 19–20:

> *Kings came, they fought,*
> *the kings of Canaan fought.*

Silence the Enemy and Avenger

> *At Taanach, by the waters of Megiddo,*
> *they took no plunder of silver.*
> *From the heavens the stars fought,*
> *from their courses they fought against Sisera.*

Notice that it says the "stars" fought from the heavens against Sisera. In the Bible, "stars," sometimes refer to angels. In addition, in verse 23, it further says:

> *'Curse Meroz,' said the angel of the Lord.*
> *'Curse its people bitterly,*
> *because they did not come to help the Lord,*
> *to help the Lord against the mighty.'*

The " . . . *angel of the Lord* . . . " was the one speaking indicating that angels participated in this battle. Sisera is the powerful commander of the army of Jabin, the King of Canaan and led a coalition of Canaanite armies. Jabin, backed by Sisera with his 900 iron chariots, had oppressed the Israelites for more than 20 years. This was why Barak, the commander of the armies of Israel, was very reluctant to go to battle against him.

In Job 38, the term "stars" is used again to symbolize angels, as we just saw in the previous verses. When God finally responds to Job's complaints, He poses a series of rhetorical questions about cosmological, geological, and wildlife phenomena to highlight Job's limited understanding and to humble him regarding his questioning of God's justice. God begins by challenging Job, *"Where were you when I laid the earth's foundation?"* (Job 38:4), and continues with imagery that includes the *"morning stars"* singing together and the *"sons of God"* shouting for joy (Job 38:7), pointing to angelic beings present at creation. This underscores God's sovereign power and Job's inability to comprehend divine purposes, let alone challenge them.

Although the angels of God participated in the battle and fought alongside the armies of Israel, Barak had to begin the battle. God did not do the fighting for them. Rather, He fought with and through them—through Barak, Deborah and the armies of Israel. God is with you in your battles but He can only fight with you and through you. Take your stand in the battle and enforce your victory.

Another account of angels joining God's people in battle is found in 2 Samuel 5:17–25. After David was anointed king over all Israel, the Philistines, likely feeling betrayed due to his former alliance with them, waged war against him. David defeated them in the initial battle, but the Philistines regrouped and attacked again in the Valley of Rephaim. David sought the Lord's guidance on how to conduct the war, and God instructed him to flank and ambush them from behind. Then, in verse 24, the Lord added a specific sign to signal the involvement of His angelic forces in the battle.

> *As soon as you hear the sound of marching*
> *in the tops of the poplar trees, move quickly,*
> *because that will mean the Lord has gone out in front of you*
> *to strike the Philistine army.*

David was not to attack until he heard the sound of marching in the tops of the poplar trees. Human armies do not march on top of trees so this marching was clearly not human and can only mean one thing. Angels were the ones doing the marching in the spiritual realm. The Lord confirmed what the sound of the marching meant when He said that, the sound of the marching means "*the Lord has gone out in front of you to strike the Philistine army.*" Therefore, angels participated in the battle to defeat the Philistine. This should give you confidence to fight your own battles because the Lord will order His angels into battle on your side.

When Satan tries to bring sickness, face him and declare God's promises for your health. If he attempts to disrupt your home, children, or business, stand firm and tell him no, standing on God's Word. You need to know God's promises for your life. Do not let the devil scare you. *The enemy you fear, fears you.* The enemy you are afraid of is, in fact, afraid of you.

Another aspect of silencing the enemy and avenger is this: God does not just want to silence your enemies through you; He also wants to use you to silence the enemies troubling other people's lives.

I was once visiting a brother-in-law in the hospital when I became deeply distressed over the condition of a man I saw there. Upon returning home, I prayed earnestly for his healing. A few days later, during another visit, a family member shared that the man had made a miraculous recovery and that the hospital had discharged him. This is what God can use you to accomplish in other people's lives through prayers.

Sometimes you are in a workplace or live in a neighborhood where there is so much moral corruption and unrighteousness and your righteous soul is vexed like Lot—2 Peter 2:8 but you feel that you cannot do anything about it and wish that God will do something. Alternatively, you see the works of darkness flourishing in a place and you desire that God will stop it. You should know that God usually does not do anything except through His people. God says " . . . *You are My battle-ax and weapons of war*"—Jeremiah 51:20. God will only act through you.

God wants to silence those enemies through you. He can only do it through you. If you will take your stand in battle, God will destroy those works of darkness.

Do you see a home ravaged by the devil? God wants to silence the enemy through you. Do you see a life messed up by the enemy? God wants to use you to silence that enemy.

In your workplace, neighborhood, village, town, or state, God wants to use you to silence the forces of darkness and hold back the hands of the evil one.

SATAN IS AN AVENGER

As God uses you to silence the enemy in people's lives, I want you to remember that the devil is an avenger. The Psalmist calls him the *enemy* and *Avenger*—Psalm 8:2. He is going to try to hit back at you. That is why you must watch your life closely and always be spiritually ready.

Let me share a story to illustrate this. One early evening during my college years, a friend and I were heading to our dorm when we noticed a young man, accompanied by two others about 50 feet away, collapsed and was dying. We rushed over, and I took hold of him, rebuking the spirit of death and commanding life to return to him. Afterward, we brought him to his room, prayed for him, and he made a full recovery.

The devil was not happy with what we did because it was a powerful deliverance. In fact, the young man who we later discovered is a Christian brother told us afterwards that he was sure that he was going to die. Because the Lord frustrated the devil's plan through us, the devil, shortly after, attacked my friend and me with fever but the Lord gave us victory. So, be on your guard but do not be afraid to make yourself available to the Lord. Even if the devil hits back, the Lord will give you victory.

GOD'S BABES AND SUCKLINGS

I want you to see something in Psalm 8:2 that is very powerful and exciting. God has a battle to fight with His enemies, but He is going to use " . . . *babes and sucklings* . . . " to silence those enemies. Following the Triumphal Entry, Jesus used the phrase to describe the crowd following Him into the temple, who hailed Him as the *"Son of David."* This adoration offended the religious authorities, who voiced their disapproval. Quoting Psalm 8:2, Jesus

PART II. KNOW YOUR ENEMY

responded, *"Have ye never read, 'Out of the mouth of babes and sucklings thou hast perfected praise?'"* (Matthew 21:16, KJV). The phrase *"babes and sucklings"* is a metaphor that affirms that we are all children to God.

In the culture of my upbringing, there exists a belief and practice that when an enemy challenges the head of a household, and the head deems the enemy inferior, he summons one of his children, whom he considers a suitable match, to confront and handle the enemy. This same principle echoes in the verse. God's greatness far surpasses the devil, who is utterly inferior, beyond any comparison. Thus, God has chosen you and me—if we are His children—to defeat the devil. We are His *"babes and sucklings,"* entrusted with this sacred task.

Let me delve deeper into the truth that God is infinitely greater than the devil and the forces of darkness, as many believers have little understanding of God's overwhelming power and preeminence while holding an exaggerated view of the devil's power. Most people, including unfortunately some believers, ignorantly expect that there will be a final confrontation between God or Jesus and the devil. There will not be because the devil is beneath God. Allow me to provide the true and clear perspective.

As I explained earlier in discussing the devil's fall at this book's outset, the devil is not, and can never be, God's equal. He would never dare challenge God directly. God assigns His angels and us, as believers, to engage in spiritual battles. In Revelation 19, when we see Jesus on a white horse leading heaven's armies, it is not to confront the devil but to defeat the Beast and his human forces. The devil is not Jesus' equal either. There will be no climactic showdown where God or Jesus battles the devil. Instead, the devil will be defeated and evil destroyed as well when a single angel binds and imprisons him for a thousand years (Revelation 20:2). Afterward, he is thrown into the lake of fire.

I want you to know that this great and powerful God of Psalm 8 commissioned you for battle. He made the heavens, the moon and the stars—verse 3—and the earth and everything in it—verses 6–8. You cannot lose. Even the devil exists to serve God's pleasure. The Bible says in Revelations 4:11

> *You are worthy, O Lord, To receive glory and honor and power;*
> *For You created all things, And by Your will they exist and were created.*
> NKJV

This God is on your side. You do not have to be afraid of the devil and his demons. God created you to be a victor and to prevail against the forces of darkness. Stand in your dominion. Do not accept the devil's lie that you cannot overcome. You must believe that you can. You will only overcome if you believe that you can.

You can defeat the schemes of the devil and his demonic forces. This is not because you are strong in yourself but because God is on your side. He is not only on your side; He is inside of you. The Scripture says:

> *You, dear children, are from God and have overcome them,*
> *because the one who is in you is greater than the one who is in the*
> *world.*
> 1 John 4:4

Sometimes, the devil will tell you that you are sick, oppressed and afflicted because you are a new believer, or that you are spiritually weak and therefore cannot win. The devil once told me this lie when I was a new believer and I fell for it. I was going through some demonic oppression at the time. I had prayed many times, believed God and confessed the Word of God but it did not stop. Therefore, the devil told me that the reason why I cannot overcome is that I was weak and that I will never overcome until I grow strong. However, this is a lie. Neither you nor I can defeat the devil in our own strength, regardless of spiritual maturity.

You do not need to grow strong; you just need to claim the divine strength that is already yours. It is available for you to embrace. As Apostle John states in 1 John 2:14, " . . . *I write to you, young men, because you are strong . . .* " He does not say you will become strong or grow into strength, but that you are—present tense. If you believe it, it is yours. Everything God has declared about you belongs to you if you believe it. The devil's lies or your circumstances do not matter.

Listen to God's declaration: It does not matter even if you consider yourself a spiritual "*babe*" or a "*suckling*"—you can silence the enemy in your life by releasing the power God has given you through your mouth. God assures that, even as a "*babe*" or "*suckling*," whatever that means to you, you can overcome. Perhaps, you are a new believer or even consider yourself an immature Christian; you can still walk in victory because you have God's power on your side. Victory comes not from your own strength but from being strong in the Lord.

The moment I grasped this revelation, my yoke was broken. I understood that I could overcome the forces of darkness by knowing how to exercise my authority. Some of you believe defeating these forces is impossible, but it is not—the devil is merely capitalizing on your ignorance. You can start dismantling the devil's works in your life by embracing this knowledge. Knowledge is power.

In the next chapter, *"Secrets of Great Strength,"* I will delve into why spiritual strength is crucial and the actions we must take to attain it. I will start by using Samson's life as an example to highlight these points, and then provide practical steps we should follow.

Chapter 6

Secrets of Great Strength

To triumph over the devil and his dark forces, you must be spiritually strong. That is why Scripture says, *"Be strong in the Lord and in his mighty power"* (Ephesians 6:10, NIV). Your strength comes from God, not physical effort, since only His spiritual power brings victory.

In Matthew 12:29 (NIV), Jesus asks, *"How can anyone enter a strong man's house and steal his possessions unless he first ties up the strong man?"* He is saying it is impossible to rob a strong man without first overpowering him and you cannot overpower him unless you are stronger. For us, this means the devil cannot harm or oppress you unless he is stronger than you are. Our strength comes from God, but you must tap into His endless, unshakable power to stand firm and be strong.

This is why Scripture declares: *"be strong in the Lord."* This phrase is an imperative, functioning as a command, advice, or exhortation. I view it as both a command and an exhortation, but primarily a command. To me, it conveys two key truths.

1. One, it is your responsibility to make yourself strong. This means that, even though the strength of the Lord is available and inexhaustible, it does not become yours except you tap into it.
2. Two, the responsibility to make yourself strong is an ongoing, continuous process. That is, you need to make yourself strong always.

The devil cannot overcome God's strength, but he can overpower you if you do not draw on God's power. Satan knows this and works hard to keep you from tapping into the Lord's strength. Many believers fall easy prey to the devil because they are spiritually weak. It is not that God's Word is not true, or that the devil has not been defeated, or that our victory in Christ is not real—it is that these believers lack spiritual strength.

The devil knows he can defeat you if he keeps you spiritually weak. If you are not strong in the Lord, you are vulnerable. You cannot beat the devil on your own strength. That is why the Bible says, *"Be strong in the Lord and in His mighty power"* (Ephesians 6:10, NIV). In the same chapter in verses 14–18, Apostle Paul shares seven ways to gain spiritual strength, seven keys to standing strong in the Lord. They are:

1. The Breastplate of *Righteousness*. This is a call for us to live right. Our salvation is free and it is by God's grace but the Bible says that grace is not a license for evil, to live self-indulgent and licentious lives.

2. The Belt of *Truth*. The Roman soldier's belt held his armor together, ready for battle. It is the first piece you need to stand strong against the devil. We need the knowledge of the truth to walk in victory.

3. The *Readiness* that comes from the gospel of peace. It is the image of a Roman soldier with his sandals on his feet ready to go into battle. This means that we must be in a state of spiritual readiness day or night. The Bible says *". . . put on the full armor of God, so that when the day of evil comes, you may be able to stand your ground, and after you have done everything, to stand"*—verse 13. We must always stay spiritually prepared and alert. Just like in physical warfare, the devil often uses surprise attacks to catch us off guard. If he strikes when you are not ready, you will not be able to resist him. Stay vigilant, spiritually tuned in, and aware of what the devil and his forces are up to. As the hymn writer so rightly puts it:

    Principalities and powers
    mustering their unseen
    arrays, waiting for thine
    unguarded hours, watch and pray

4. The Shield of *Faith*. We need faith in God and in His Word to win. This is our defense against the devil's weapon of fear.

5. The Helmet of *Salvation*. This means that you must be saved. Our salvation through Jesus Christ is what qualifies us to share in the victory

of Christ. 1 John 5:4 says, *"for everyone born of God overcomes the world. This is the victory that has overcome the world, even our faith."* Only those who are born of God, who are believers can, and will overcome the world.

6. The Sword of the Spirit is the *Word of God*. You must know and keep God's Word deep in your heart and spirit. Knowing the Word is your shield against the devil's weapons of lies, ignorance, and fear.

7. Lastly, *Praying* in the spirit. You need to maintain a regular and active prayer life. In Matthew chapter 6, before Jesus taught the model prayer, He said in verse 5, *"when you pray,"* not "if you pray." Prayer is not optional for Christians—it is a vital necessity. These are not prayers you just recite, follow from a script, or say by rote, but heartfelt, direct conversations with God. Any believer who does not make prayer a daily habit will face a life marked by defeat.

I believe that we can sum up these components of the armor of God into three key principles: *Righteous Living, Knowledge of the Word of God*, and a *Regular Prayer Life*. Righteous Living is our breastplate of righteousness. The Word of God is our Belt of Truth, Shield of Faith and Sword of the Spirit. Lastly, a Regular Prayer Life is praying in the Spirit on all occasions. Let us examine each of these in detail.

LIVING RIGHT IS YOUR SUPERPOWER

I believe a key secret to great spiritual strength is living a righteous life. I received this revelation from studying Samson's story in Judges Chapter 16. Samson, a prominent judge, tragically fell short of his potential due to his personal shortcomings.

Samson Fallen Hero

Samson's story is tragic and tells of a hero who fell from greatness. When the Philistine lords put out a contract on his life in the Book of Judges chapter 16, they recruited Delilah, the seductress, to " . . . *find out where his great strength lies, and by what means we may overpower him, that we may bind him to afflict him . . .* "—verse 5. By the way, this chapter's heading "*Secrets of Great Strength*" is taken from this Samson's story.

The Philistines understood that they could not defeat Samson or overpower him without first exploiting his vulnerability. This prompted the Philistine lords to task Delilah with uncovering the secret (or source) of his immense strength. Delilah skillfully manipulated him, coaxing Samson into revealing the key to his power. It is astonishing how foolishly people can act when they think they are in "love," which is often merely lust. You would expect Samson, aware that Delilah was a Philistine and that the Philistines were his sworn enemies, to be wary or at least question her motives. Yet, tragically, he naively went along with her.

Through persistent nagging and seduction, Delilah eventually persuaded Samson to disclose that cutting his hair would strip him of his strength. I suspect her seduction likely involved alcohol and sex—a perilous combination that has long been a tool in the devil's arsenal to ruin countless men and women. It was only after Delilah cut his hair, causing his strength to leave him in verse 19, that the Philistines could overpower and bind him. They had tried three times prior but failed until Samson revealed his secret. Be careful about sharing your secrets, if you have any. Even with loved ones, only confide in those you can absolutely trust to keep them safe.

There are lessons that we can draw from the life of Samson:

1. *The devil cannot defeat you except he first takes away your strength.* The devil's time-tested, age-old trick is to weaken a child of God before oppressing or afflicting them. He first strips away their spiritual strength. Satan does not come up with new schemes—he sticks to this same old tactic. The Bible says " . . . *there is nothing new under the sun*"—Ecclesiastes 1:9. This is why understanding the schemes of the devil is crucial to defeating him. Samson's power came from keeping his hair uncut, as he was called to be a Nazirite his whole life. His hair symbolized God's anointing on him, the source of his strength—Judges 13:4–5.

2. *Beware with whom you associate.* You must realize that not everyone who enters your life, or whom you welcome in, has your best interests at heart. The devil may have enlisted them, just as he used Delilah, to destroy you or wreck your life. This is why young people, in particular, must be careful about choosing their friends or romantic partners. Many have derailed their lives and shattered their dreams for the future by associating or building relationships with the wrong individuals.

3. *Do not be a lone-ranger.* Samson was born to lead, yet he lived as a loner. Unlike other judges like Gideon, Barak, or Jephthah, he never built friendships or gathered supporters around him. One of the devil's tricks to destroy someone is to isolate them from loved ones—those who care and can offer wise advice or warn of dangers. We see Samson ignored his parents' counsel when they urged him not to marry the Philistine woman in Judges 14:1–4. It is often observed in some societies that one partner—sadly, frequently men—harms or even kills their spouse or romantic partner, whether in marriage or sinful relationships like fornication or adultery. Usually, the controlling person, who later turns violent, starts by cutting their partner off from friends and loved ones. We all need people in our lives who can offer guidance or advice, especially in romantic relationships where so-called "love" often blinds us, but is really just lust in disguise. Our friends or loved ones often spot dangers we miss. Do not be someone who brushes off advice or ignores warnings. You do not have to follow every suggestion, but you will help yourself greatly by not dismissing or overlooking them. Scripture says, " . . . *in a multitude of counselors there is safety*" (Proverbs 24:6). You do not need to follow every bit of advice, but you can gain from listening. Getting counsel from various sources opens your eyes to new viewpoints and helps you see the risks in your choices. A crucial word, especially for young women and women everywhere: never let a man cut you off from your family or friends. Steer clear of controlling relationships where a man pushes you to sever ties with those who truly care. Do not trust a man who says he loves you but isolates you from your loved ones.

4. *Flee anyone who urges you to do something wrong to prove your love for them.* Delilah pressured Samson to demonstrate his love by revealing the secret of his strength, saying in Judges 16:15, " . . . *How can you say, 'I love you' when you won't confide in me?*" It is astonishing what people will do when they claim to be in love. Yet, I urge, especially young people: anyone who demands you prove your love by acting against your best interests or doing something wrong does not truly love you. Run from them.

Samson possessed superhuman strength, a true-life superhero, and not the caricatures of sci-fi movies or TV. To the Philistines, he was a menace and a nightmare, making his elimination a priority. Like some men, women were his weakness, a vulnerability the Philistines recognized and exploited by enlisting Delilah to bring him down. Delilah's task was to uncover the secret of his extraordinary strength. She pursued this goal brazenly, asking him outright, " . . . *Please tell me where your great strength lies, and with what you may be bound to afflict you*"—Judges 16:6 (NKJV).

Three times, Samson lied to Delilah on what the secret of his great strength was. Nevertheless, he finally caved in under her unrelenting nagging and cajoling. See what Samson says in verse 17:

> *. . . No razor has ever been used on my head, he said,*
> *because I have been a Nazirite set apart to God since birth.*
> *if my head were shaved, my strength would leave me,*
> *and I would become as weak as any other man.*

What is the revelation here? Samson's hair—his seven locks—was the symbol of his consecration as a Nazirite—Numbers 6:7. As long as the hair was unshaved or uncut, his consecration remained, and his strength remained. What this means is that the Philistines would never be able to subdue him except they destroy his consecration. Moreover, the way to destroy his consecration was to shave his head.

It is probable that Samson violated his Nazirite vow by drinking wine and was likely intoxicated, as it is hard to imagine Delilah weaving the seven locks of his hair into a loom or shaving his head without him noticing. As a Nazirite, Samson was forbidden from consuming wine throughout his life. In fact, this restriction was so strict that the angel instructed his mother to abstain from wine during her pregnancy with him (Judges 13:4). However, I believe Samson compromised his consecration by drinking alcohol and was probably under its influence when Delilah performed those acts.

As soon as Delilah shaved his head, his strength left him. The Lord said to me, "*This is the secret of great strength. As long as you live a holy life, keeping your heart pure, no devil can overpower you.*"

I want you to see something else. Samson's strength was actually of the Lord. In verse 19, the Bible says " . . . *his strength left him*" after his hair was shaved. However, in verse 20, using a similar expression, the Bible says that Samson did not know that the " . . . *Lord had left him.*" The presence of the Lord in his life was actually the reason for his great strength. Consequently, as soon as he lost his consecration, the presence of the Lord departed from him and he became like any other man.

The story of Samson offers numerous lessons and serves as a cautionary tale for generations, particularly for today. Samson resembles modern ministers, pastors, prophets, and evangelists who misuse their God-given anointing and gifts for self-gratification. God appointed Samson to deliver the Israelites from the Philistines, yet during his 20 years as a judge, he accomplished little of this mission. Instead, he wielded his power for personal vendettas against the Philistines, such as when he burned their fields in Judges Chapter 15 after they killed the woman he intended to marry and her father.

I watch a bit of crime TV, and I have been appalled and saddened by crimes committed by so-called pastors. There was one where a male pastor was carrying on an adulterous relationship with a vulnerable female who needed his protection and help, all with the knowledge and cooperation of his wife. He impregnated her and this pastor and his wife were going to perpetrate a lie on the church body by claiming that this female was just a surrogate. He also tried unsuccessfully to sell and justify a polygamous lifestyle to his church. When the female refused to give up the baby after giving birth, he killed and buried her in his backyard. He later claimed that the woman had attacked him and he only acted in self-defense.

There was another where another married pastor was committing adultery with the wife of his best friend. He wanted her so much that he killed his best friend so that he can continue to be with her.

Many pastors or church leaders abuse their position and calling for sexual gratification, coaxing or coercing sex from church members or followers. This echoes the actions of Eli's sons, Hophni and Phinehas, who slept with women who came to worship at the temple (1 Samuel 2:22). Their fate is well known: God allowed the Philistines to destroy them in battle (1 Samuel 4:17). Similarly, Christian leaders and pastors have faced premature death through illnesses or ruined themselves through personal tragedies.

The Bible shows us that there is a connection between personal righteousness and physical health. Sometimes when people are sick, it is because of some unconfessed or persistent sin in their lives.

Apostle James tells believers to call for the elders of the church to pray for the sick and in James 5:14 says *"And the prayer of faith will save the sick, and the Lord will raise him up. And if he has committed sins, he will be forgiven."* The "if" means that sin is sometimes the cause or vector of sickness. When it is the case, God will not only heal the sick person but He will also forgive their sin.

After healing the man at the pool of Bethesda, who had been ill for 38 years, Jesus said to him, *" . . . See, you have been made well. Sin no more, lest a worse thing come upon you"*—John 5:14. Jesus is letting us know that this man got sick in the first place because of some sin. In healing him, Jesus also forgave the sin.

From Job's story, we know the devil can inflict sickness (Job 2:7), though in Job's case, it was not due to sin but because God permitted it to test him. Still, it demonstrates that demonic forces can cause some illnesses. Similarly, Jesus states in Luke 13 that Satan had bound a woman with rheumatoid arthritis for 18 years, further confirming this truth.

Samson's story illustrates how a single wrong choice can spiral into further mistakes. He began by insisting on marrying a Philistine woman despite his parents' objections, then progressed to sleeping with a prostitute, and later took Delilah as a sexual partner. Human life is filled with similar tales, where one poor decision leads to a chain of increasingly wrong choices.

These wrong choices might involve marrying an unbeliever or engaging in a romantic or sexual relationship with one. People often rationalize such decisions with various excuses and justifications. However, you must understand that fornication or sex outside of marriage remains a sin, and no excuse will hold up before a Holy God. Apostle Paul declares, *"Now the works of the flesh are evident, which are: adultery, fornication, uncleanness, lewdness"*—Galatians 5:19 (KJV). He further warns, *"Do not be deceived, God is not mocked; for whatever a man sows, that he will also reap."*—Galatians 6:7 (KJV). Living in sexual immorality carries consequences, and you cannot deceive or outwit a Holy God.

God has a purpose in prohibiting sex before marriage. Sex is a wonderful gift from God, but once experienced, it creates a strong desire to repeat it. Those who engage in premarital sex may find it difficult to stop, even if they wish to, much like opening the mythical Pandora's Box.

We see teenagers, some as young as 13, beginning to engage in sexual activity. Society has grown increasingly promiscuous, often viewing virginity as outdated or uncool. In fact, adolescents or young adults, particularly young men, who claim to be virgins are sometimes suspected or accused of being homosexuals. Choosing to remain a virgin until marriage honors God and you should be very proud of your choice because God is very proud of you.

God's wisdom in commanding us to wait until marriage for sex lies in its ability to restrain the sexual impulse, which, once unleashed, becomes challenging to control. The consequences of young people engaging in premarital sex are evident all around us:

- We observe it in the widespread problem of infertility and childlessness that is afflicting societies, where individuals who have engaged in years of premarital sex, used birth control medications, or undergone abortions struggle to conceive due to weakened or damaged reproductive systems. While married women may also use contraceptives, they typically do so to avoid additional pregnancies after having the children they desired.

- We see it in the many children born out of wedlock and placed for adoption because their young parents are unable to care for them. While some argue that adoption benefits married couples or people who cannot have biological children, this does not excuse the promiscuity that leads to so many children being given up for adoption.

- We see it in the number of unwanted pregnancies that women abort and in the proliferation of abortion clinics where the owners essentially trade in the lives of unborn babies.

- We see it in the number of young people, especially young women, whose hopes and dreams for the future are shattered because they got pregnant. Many are unable to go to college and end up in dead-end or low-wage jobs or worse, become at risk for depression or substance abuse.

- We see it in the problem of Sexually Transmitted Disease (STD) from people having multiple sexual partners, which may be a cause of infertility.

Samson's story is also about redemption; showing that God can forgive us no matter how far we have strayed. God restored him before his death. However, do not mistake this as permission to persist in a sexually immoral lifestyle, expecting forgiveness and redemption later. You may not have the chance to repent, so you must turn from sin today.

In Numbers chapter 23, Balaam, the Moabite prophet—more accurately described as a sorcerer—recognized that the Israelites were invincible as long as God was with them. The Moabite king had hired him to curse the Israelites because they were afraid of them. They feared them specifically because of their God—Jehovah. For the same reason, *the enemy you fear, fears you*. Balaam understood that no sorcery, divination, or enchantment (verse 23) and no curse (verse 8) could succeed against them while God remained their protector.

Therefore, the Bible says that Balaam taught Balak, the Moabite king to cause the Israelites to sin. How, you may ask? The Lord tells us, in Revelations 2:14 that Balak enticed them to commit fornication or sexual immorality and to commit idolatry by eating food sacrificed to idols. Society now considers the word *"fornication"* to be politically incorrect and considers it old-fashioned to say that people should not engage in premarital sex. However, you must understand that our God is "old-fashioned" in the sense that He remains unchanging, and engaging in premarital sex or sex with someone who is not your spouse is still a sin.

In numbers 23:21 (KJV), Balaam prophesied this: *"He [God] hath not beheld iniquity in Jacob, neither hath he seen perverseness in Israel."* Therefore, he says, *"... the Lord his God is with him, and the shout of the king is among them."* Because God's presence was with them, Balaam went further to say in verses 22 and 23 that they have the strength of a unicorn, and that no enchantment or divination will succeed against them. In the ancient Near East, single-horned creatures, like wild oxen or mythical beasts like the unicorn, symbolized strength and divinity.

I want you to know that if the presence of the Lord is with you, you have great strength and the key to that great strength is a holy life. We cannot live the way Samson lived and expect not to be vulnerable to demonic oppressions and afflictions.

You must understand that your greatest defense against the devil is living right according to God's standards of morality, not society's. It is your breastplate of righteousness. I want you to know that if you walk in purity in your heart, in your thoughts, in your imagination and in your actions, no devil or demon can overpower or subdue you. This is not to say that we do not sin but that when we do, we acknowledge it and confess and/or repent of it.

Your faith, prayers, and fasting will not be enough to shield you from the powers of darkness if you do not live right. The Philistines overcame Samson because he neglected this vital aspect. You may have strong faith and be devoted to prayer, but you must combine these with righteous living.

Our Lord Jesus declares, *"... the prince of this world cometh, and hath nothing in me"*—John 14:30 (KJV). The Living Bible renders it, *"... he has no power over me."* The devil can have no power or authority over you unless he finds something in you. Examine your lifestyle.

THE SEED OF GOD'S LIFE

Many Christian believers are spiritually weak because they give little time and attention to read, study, and meditate on the Word of God. Sometimes, you see a believer who will not bother to open his or her Bible a whole day, a whole week, or even longer. You find Christians who read the Bible as a novel or in a whole day, may read just a few verses and they do it in a hurry.

Some Christians reflect this lax attitude towards the Word of God by the fact that they do not have a hard-copy complete Bible comprising the Old and New Testaments but just a New Testament Bible or may not even have a Bible at all. This is most unfortunate.

You observe a situation where Christian believers carry about torn and worn out Bibles with missing chapters and they will not care to replace them. They spend money on the latest fashion, electronics, or video games but not on buying or replacing their Bibles. Of course, now especially in modern societies, you do not have to carry a hard copy Bible. There are free Bible apps for a number of popular translations and if there is not one available for your translation, you can buy one for little money. Yet, there are believers who still do not have a Bible. This, to say the least, is appalling.

All these attitudes reflect a lack of value for and appreciation of the Word of God. The devil is pleased with a Christian who does not spend time with, or is too busy to stay with the Word. This way, he can keep him or her a spiritual weakling. One dear minister and older brother-in-law, says, *"The level of life you are operating in is determined by the level of the Word in your life."*

The Word of God is the seed of God's life. 1 Peter 1:23 (NIV) says *"For you have been born again, not of perishable seed, but of imperishable, through the living and enduring word of God."* The Word of God is the seed of God's life in us. Therefore, the level of the Word of God that you have in your spirit determines the level of God's life that you have.

The reason why some Christians are regularly or always sick is that the level of God's life in them is low. As a result, they are spiritually weak. It is for this same reason that they are afflicted and oppressed.

I found out that the human spirit behaves in much the same way as the human body. Like you need physical food to sustain your physical life, so you also need spiritual food to sustain your spirit. The spiritual food is the Word of God. In Matthew 4:4 (NKJV), Jesus says, *"Man shall not live by bread alone, but by every word that proceeds from the mouth of God."* Apostle Peter also says in 1 Peter 2:2 (NIV) *"Like newborn babies, crave pure spiritual milk, so that by it you may grow up in your salvation."* You need the Word of God for your spiritual nourishment and growth. You need it to sustain your spiritual life, the life of God within you.

In John chapter 6 Jesus told the Jews in verse 53 *"Very truly I tell you, unless you eat the flesh of the Son of Man and drink his blood, you have no life in you."* They did not understand what He meant and were confused and even annoyed because they thought that He was referring to His physical body and blood. In fact, some of Jesus' disciples turned back from following Him.

It was not until 10 verses later, that we come to understand that Jesus was NOT referring to His physical body and blood. In verse 63, Jesus followed up by saying *"It is the Spirit who gives life; the flesh profits nothing. The words that I speak to you are spirit, and they are life."* Jesus is saying that eating His flesh and drinking His blood was just a metaphor because *"the flesh profits nothing."* Instead, the words, which He has spoken, are the spirit that gives life. The Bible is the Word of God.

Everyone knows, and I doubt anyone would argue, that we eat food to gain physical strength and energy, as Ecclesiastes 10:17 (NKJV) says, *"Blessed are you, O land, when your king is the son of nobles, and your princes feast at the proper time—for strength and not for drunkenness!"* We eat to stay strong physically. In the same way, we need spiritual food for spiritual strength, and that food is God's Word. If you do not spend time feeding on the Word of God, you will stay spiritually weak, making it easy for the forces of darkness to overpower you.

In my early twenties, the Lord started teaching me this lesson through a vivid experience. In a dream, someone stole something that was mine. Instead of fighting to reclaim it, I cried, feeling powerless. I woke up right away, shaken and troubled. Your dreams often reflect your spiritual state. If you see yourself being beaten, running from, or crying before your enemies in dreams, it is a clear sign of spiritual weakness and defeat.

I realized that the dream I had revealed some kind of oppression, and I wondered why I could not fight back. The Lord told me it was because I was spiritually weak, and my weakness came from having too little of His Word in my life. At that time, I would often only read and reflect on a single verse or a few verses of the Bible for an entire day.

Consuming minimal amounts of food, such as one or two spoonful of cereal per day, will not provide the necessary nutrients and caloric intake required to sustain physical strength. Adequate nutrition is essential for generating and maintaining the energy and muscle function needed for physical performance and overall health. In the same way, if you do not eat enough of the Word of God, you cannot be spiritually healthy or generate adequate spiritual strength.

I can literally feel when my spirit is undernourished or I am spiritually hungry. I feel it in my body and I feel it when I perform spiritual activities like praying or fasting. I have developed this sense from years of practicing feeding my spirit with the Word of God. Therefore, whenever I am undernourished, I feel it.

Let me expand on the role and impact of our spirits on our physical life. The health of our spirits, many times, determine how we react to life's complications or difficulties or how we perform in them:

1. How you react to, or perform in, negative situations oftentimes is indicative of the state of, or the health of, your spirit. The Bible says, *"If you faint in the day of adversity, Your strength is small."*—Proverbs 24:10. This is not saying that you cannot get discouraged. Even great men and women of God (Moses, Elijah, John the Baptist, Jeremiah, etc.) got discouraged sometimes but they often express it privately and do not infect others with their doubts. There are those who have abandoned the faith because they had neglected their spiritual health. This is what Jesus was saying when He talked about the wise and foolish builders—Matthew 7:24–27. We all go through the same difficulties or struggles in life but how we react or perform in them depends on what we have built our lives on.

2. Joyfulness is a fruit of the Holy Spirit. Apostle Paul says, *"the fruit of the Spirit is love, joy . . . "*—Galatians 5:22 (NKJV). *Happiness is a mind or mental thing but joy is a condition of the spirit.* It is why someone may be going through stuff and understand mentally that things are not okay but can remain joyful. The Holy Spirit communicates joy to our spirits. When the 70 disciples returned and reported to Jesus that the demons submitted to them in His name, the Bible says that Jesus rejoiced in the Spirit—Luke 10:21. If you lack joyfulness in your life, it may be because you are spiritually unhealthy.

3. Fasting is a spiritual exercise or activity, whatever you want to call it, that every Christian should engage in for if not for any other reason but that our Lord Jesus Christ did it. Jesus fasted 40 days and nights before He started His ministry—Matthew 4:2. Jesus is our ultimate

example. Although not recorded, I believe that He must have fasted at other times during His 3 ½ years ministry. There are physical benefits to fasting, like to lose weight, to receive healing, etc. but we fast primarily to express humility before God and our dependence on Him. Fasting can be tough on the human body, especially for young people, because they may have more food cravings than adults may have. Therefore, after just a few hours, the human body becomes physically weak and people are not able to do much. I have found that nourishing my spirit well ahead and during a fasting period, whether it is 1 day, 3 days, 7 days or more with the Word of God helps me get through it. Because my spirit is well fed and nourished, it helps to sustain my physical body.

4. Praying is an essential requirement of the Christian life. We need to make it an integral part of our daily routine. We are required to pray, this is why Jesus taught us to pray and said *"And when you pray . . . "*—Matthew 6:5. He says *"when"* you pray and not *"if"* you pray. Praying is not an optional activity that we do if we like it. However, if your spirit is weak and unhealthy, you will struggle with praying. If you find yourself distracted during private or public praying and are not able to concentrate, it may be that your spirit is in a weakened state. An energized spirit helps you to focus and remain active during praying.

5. A healthy spirit is important for our physical health. It helps both to prevent sickness and to enable quick recovery. Apostle John, praying for the prosperity of the church, prays in 3 John 1:2 that believers will *" . . . be in health, just as your soul prospers."* Apostle John, in praying for the physical health of believers, makes a connection between the health of the body and of the spirit when he says, *"as your soul prospers."* Proverbs 18:14 also says *"The spirit of a man will sustain him in sickness, But who can bear a broken spirit?"* A healthy spirit creates the condition for quick healing and recovery. If you are struggling to recover from, or are susceptible to frequent sickness or illness, it may be that your spirit is weak, undernourished, or malnourished.

We need spiritual health and strength to perform optimally in life. Some believers always need healing and deliverance ministry; they experience oppression in their dreams and cannot fight back because they are spiritually weak. The Bible says, *"No one can contend with someone who is stronger"*—Ecclesiastes 6:10 (NIV).

Stop being spiritually weak. Spend enough time feeding on God's Word, and you will grow spiritually strong. You need the Word to stand firm. *Do not let the devil use you as a punching bag. Be a victor, not a victim.*

PRAYER BUILDS SPIRITUAL MUSCLES

Keeping a regular and effective prayer life is another way to develop spiritual strength. Prayer is a spiritual exercise that helps you to develop tough and strong spiritual muscles. You need this exercise to keep fit spiritually.

Remember that the human spirit behaves in similar ways to the human body. It is just not enough to eat well; you need to exercise your body. In the same way, you need not only to eat well spiritually, but you also need to exercise your spirit. Praying is the way to do this.

Imagine a situation where someone eats very well but lives a sedentary lifestyle. They stay on their bed or sofa; they do not move about and do not engage in any activity. What will happen to such a person? They will become physically dull and their muscles will atrophy from inactivity. It is the same with our spirits. The Bible says in Isaiah 40:31 (KJV):

> *But they that wait upon the Lord*
> *shall renew their strength;*
> *they shall mount up with wings as eagles;*
> *they shall run, and not be weary;*
> *and they shall walk, and not faint.*

One way to wait on the Lord is through praying. When you pray, you draw strength from the Lord. Earlier in Isaiah 40:29 (NIV), the Bible says "*He [God] gives strength to the weary and increases the power of the weak.*" If you want or need spiritual strength, you must pray. Spiritual strength is available to you. You must combine feeding on the word of God with praying.

In concluding this topic on the need to be spiritually strong, I want to encourage you to be careful and to take your spiritual life seriously. Whenever you begin to get too busy, or find excuses, or are too much in a hurry to pray or read the Bible, watch it. The devil may be setting you up. Keep your heart pure as well.

The devil knows that as long as you are spiritually strong and agile, he cannot beat you. Therefore, he is always scheming to distract you from spiritual priorities such as praying and reading the Word of God. Do not pray as if you are merely observing some religious obligation or routine.

Pray because you need it and because you understand it to be so. Set your priorities right. Give attention to the Word of God because it is your very life.

In the next chapter, I will share some thoughts on fasting, which is practiced by most religions. For us, believers though, it is not a religious ritual but a vital spiritual activity. My goal in the chapter is to show that while it is an important activity, it is not a spiritual weapon like some ministers teach or some believe.

Chapter 7

What of Fasting?

YOU MAY HAVE WONDERED why I did not include fasting as a secret of great spiritual strength. If you have been a believer for some time or come from a traditional Christian background, you may have learned—or even taught others—that fasting is necessary to win spiritual battles or that it serves as a spiritual weapon. *While fasting is undoubtedly a valuable spiritual practice and a powerful complement to prayer, the Bible does not describe it as a weapon.*

It is okay if you disagree with me on this, but fasting is about drawing closer to God, not directly fighting the devil. That said, by humbling ourselves and becoming more spiritually alert through fasting, we might be better positioned to resist the enemy and walk in obedience. To understand fasting's true role and purpose, let us look at what the Old and New Testaments teach about the subject.

OLD TESTAMENT FASTING

Let us examine several significant examples involving God's people to understand how fasting was practiced in the Old Testament.

One well-known instance of community fasting occurred when Ezra proclaimed a fast at the river Ahava (Ezra 8:21–23). He asked all the exiles traveling with him to Jerusalem to fast and humble themselves before God. The purpose was to seek God's protection for their journey through hostile territories. Ezra admitted he was ashamed to request a military escort from the king, choosing instead to seek divine help.

Ezra also engaged in a personal fast in response to the people's unfaithfulness—specifically, their intermarriage with foreigners in violation of God's commands (Ezra 9:5). This fast, likely a single day, was an expression of deep sorrow and repentance.

Similarly, Nehemiah fasted upon hearing about the broken walls and burned gates of Jerusalem (Nehemiah 1:4). Though the exact duration is unclear, he fasted and prayed *"for many days,"* seeking God's favor as he prepared to request permission from the king to return and rebuild the city (Nehemiah 1:11).

Queen Esther called for a three-day fast among all the Jews in Susa when a royal decree threatened their extermination (Esther 4:15–17). She, her maids, and the entire Jewish community fasted before she approached the king uninvited—a move that could have cost her life. Like Nehemiah, Esther fasted to seek divine favor before confronting a powerful ruler.

Daniel also fasted and prayed with great intensity as he sought God to fulfill His promise to restore Israel after 70 years of exile, as prophesied by Jeremiah (Daniel 9:2–3).

King David fasted when his child, born from his adulterous affair with Bathsheba, became gravely ill (2 Samuel 12:15–17). Although God had already declared through the prophet Nathan that the child would die (2 Samuel 12:14), David hoped his fasting and prayers might change the outcome. However, the child died; fasting did not change the outcome.

The most notable example of prolonged fasting in the Old Testament was by Moses, who fasted twice for 40 days and nights while receiving the Ten Commandments from God (Deuteronomy 9:9, 18). During each period, Moses neither ate bread nor drank water, as he remained in God's presence on Mount Sinai, enveloped by His glory.

These examples reveal that fasting in the Old Testament was always directed toward God—whether to seek His protection, favor, intervention, or forgiveness. It was a form of deep spiritual communion, marked by humility and dependence on God.

FASTING IS NOT A WEAPON

Fasting is often portrayed as a spiritual weapon. However, neither the Bible nor Jesus teaches this. Apostle Paul does not list fasting among the weapons of our warfare in Ephesians chapter 6, and the other Apostles do not even mention it. Let us examine fasting in the New Testament, which contains relatively few references to fasting and offers limited teaching or detailed examples, though a few notable instances exist.

The leaders of the church in Antioch, including the apostles Barnabas and Paul, were fasting when the Holy Spirit spoke to them about their missionary calling (Acts 13:2–3).

Paul fasted for three days following his encounter with Jesus on the road to Damascus, before Ananias came to restore his sight (Acts 9:9). Later, during the perilous sea voyage to Rome, Paul also fasted for at least part of the journey (Acts 27:21–27).

Cornelius, a Roman centurion, was fasting when an angel of God appeared to him and instructed him to summon Peter, who was in Joppa at the time (Acts 10:30).

The most well-known fasting account in the New Testament is that of Jesus Christ, especially as described in Luke 4. Let us examine His fast for insights. Matthew records that Jesus was led by the Spirit into the wilderness where He was tempted (Matthew 4:1). Matthew's account seems to indicate that the temptations came after the 40 days of fasting (Matthew 4:2–3), but Mark 1:13 and Luke 4:2 clarify that Jesus was tempted throughout the entire 40-day fast.

You might have believed or been taught that Jesus fasted to receive the power of the Holy Spirit. However, this is not accurate. Luke 4:1 states, *"Jesus, full of the Holy Spirit, left the Jordan and was led by the Spirit into the wilderness."* Jesus was already filled with the Holy Spirit—and thus already empowered—before He entered the wilderness.

Some might point to Luke 4:14, which says, *"Then Jesus returned in the power of the Spirit to Galilee . . . "* as evidence that Jesus gained power from fasting. But if that were true, it would imply that Jesus somehow lost the Holy Spirit's power during those 40 days and had to regain it by fasting—an idea inconsistent with Scripture. Jesus Himself revealed that the only time He lost power was when He healed or performed miracles—something He was not doing in the wilderness. We see this in Mark 5:30 and Luke 8:46, where He said, *" . . . I perceived power going out from Me"* after the woman who had a flow of blood for twelve years touched Him.

The Bible clearly teaches that we receive power from the Holy Spirit: *"But you shall receive power when the Holy Spirit has come upon you"* (Acts 1:8, NKJV). Being filled with the Holy Spirit means being filled with power. The apostles—Peter, John, and others—were only able to perform miracles after "... *they were all filled with the Holy Spirit*..." on the Day of Pentecost (Acts 2:4).

In addition, *the temptation of Jesus reveals an important truth: fasting itself is not a spiritual weapon.* First, Satan was not deterred by Jesus' fasting—otherwise, he would not have dared to tempt Him. I have faced Satan's temptations many times during my own fasts, just as many other believers have. Second, Jesus did not overcome Satan by fasting but by speaking the Word of God. We must recognize this essential truth if we are to walk in spiritual victory. I expand on this later in the chapter. However, if you believe that fasting is a spiritual weapon, that is your personal conviction. It is not a matter for dispute.

Apostle Paul mentioned fasting in the context of husbands and wives in 1 Corinthians 7:5, but there is no direct teaching about fasting in the writings of Paul or the other apostles—Peter, John, James, and Jude do not even mention it. Therefore, let us turn to what Jesus Himself taught about fasting.

Principles of Fasting

Jesus taught two key principles about fasting. First, how we should appear to others when we fast. Second, that fasting is a personal choice we undertake as we find necessary.

First, in Matthew 6:16–18, Jesus instructed that when we fast, we should not make it obvious to others or seek their praise. Instead, He said we should make our faces appear normal—so that no one notices we are fasting. Fasting is a private matter between us and God, and God, who sees what is done in secret, will reward us openly.

This does not mean we should avoid participating in church or group fasts where others are aware. Nor does it mean that family or close friends will not know we are fasting, as sometimes it is impossible to hide. Jesus' point is that fasting should never be done for show or public commendation, because such fasting receives no reward from God.

Second, Jesus taught that fasting is a personal decision. The disciples of John the Baptist and the Pharisees asked Him why His disciples did not fast as they did. The account in Luke 5:33–39 addresses this question.

They asked, "*Why do the disciples of John fast often and make prayers, and likewise those of the Pharisees, but yours eat and drink?*" (verse 33).

What of Fasting?

Jesus responded by addressing three important questions for believers: Why do we fast? When do we fast? In addition, how often should we fast?

Regarding *why we fast*, Jesus used a rhetorical question: *"Can you make the friends of the bridegroom fast while the bridegroom is with them?"* (verse 34). He implied it would be inappropriate for the bridegroom's friends to fast during the ceremony—they should be celebrating instead. Jesus, the Bridegroom (John 3:28–29), was indicating that His disciples had no need to fast while He was with them. They would fast after His ascension when they would need His intervention. The primary purpose of fasting is to seek God's help, as we see repeatedly in the Old Testament. Additionally, fasting strengthens and energizes our spirits.

For the question of *when we fast*, Jesus said, *"But the days will come when the bridegroom will be taken away from them; then they will fast in those days"* (verse 35). This suggests that fasting's timing is a matter of personal discretion. The fact that John's disciples and the Pharisees fasted simultaneously indicates they likely followed a religious calendar—Zechariah 8:19 mentions fasts in the 4th, 5th, 7th, and 10th months. Although the Bible does not explicitly say John's disciples observed this calendar, their synchronized fasting implies they did. Many nominal Christians fast during Lent, but Jesus clearly taught that we, His disciples, are not obligated to follow such religious regulations. Therefore, the timing of fasting is a personal decision, guided by individual need. However, this does not mean that fasting during Lent is wrong.

Regarding *how often we fast*, Jesus linked this to the question of when. Frequency should come from personal choice, not religious obligation or calendar mandates. This does not exclude participating in church or communal fasts. However, how often you fast—weekly, monthly, or otherwise—is up to you.

To emphasize this shift toward personal choice, Jesus used two analogies: patching an old garment with new cloth and pouring new wine into old wineskins (verses 36–39). He was introducing a new teaching that diverged from longstanding traditions, which the religious leaders would struggle to accept. As He said, *" . . . no one, having drunk old wine, immediately desires new; for he says, 'The old is better.'"* Whatever your personal convictions about fasting may be, they are valid—so long as you do not turn them into doctrine or seek to impose them on other believers.

PART II. KNOW YOUR ENEMY

FASTING AND SPIRITUAL POWER

Is fasting required to cast out demons, or does it impart any spiritual power beyond what we receive through prayer, speaking God's Word, and living righteously? No—Scripture does not support that view. Some might say, how about Matthew and Mark recording that Jesus said that some kind of demons cannot be cast out " . . . *except by prayer and fasting*"—Matthew 17:21 and Mark 9:29? Let us examine this.

In the story leading up to verse 21, Jesus had just returned from the Mount of Transfiguration when a distraught father came to Him and begged Him to cure his son. Jesus first expressed His displeasure that His disciples could not cast out the demon and then healed the son by casting out the demon.

The disciples then came privately to Jesus and asked Him why they could not cast out the demon. Jesus said in verse 20 that it was because of their unbelief. However, some Bible translations added that Jesus also said that the kind of demon could only be cast out through prayer and fasting.

> *However, this kind does not go out except by prayer and fasting.*
> Matthew 17:21 (NKJV)

> *So He said to them, "This kind can come out by nothing but prayer and fasting."*
> Mark 9:29 (NKJV)

I noted above that some Bible translations did not include these verses to point out that some New Testament translations, depending on the manuscripts they were based on, did not include these verses or not in entirety. For example, the NIV did not include Matthew 17:21 at all and did not include " . . . *and fasting*" of Mark 9:29. Let me explain why.

New Testament Bible translations are typically based on one or more of three primary Greek manuscript traditions: the Critical Text, the Textus Receptus, and the Majority Text.

The *Critical Text*, exemplified by the Nestle-Aland and United Bible Societies editions (collectively known as the NU-Text), is a scholarly reconstruction of the original New Testament text. *It draws primarily from early manuscripts*, particularly those of the Alexandrian text-type, such as Codex Sinaiticus and Codex Vaticanus, which are among the oldest surviving manuscripts, often dated to the 4th century. These manuscripts, frequently associated with Egypt due to their preservation there, are prioritized for their age and quality.

The *Textus Receptus* ("Received Text") refers to a series of Greek New Testament texts compiled by Erasmus, a Dutch theologian in the 16th century, based on small number of late Byzantine manuscripts—typically between 6 and 12. It served as the foundation for translations like the KJV and NKJV and was widely accepted in early Protestant circles. However, modern scholars view it as less reliable because of its limited manuscript base (6–12 manuscripts) and the inclusion of later textual additions.

The *Majority Text* is similar to the *Textus Receptus* but is based on the majority of existing Greek manuscripts—over 5,000, most of which are Byzantine and date from after the 5th century. It emphasizes the number of agreeing manuscripts rather than the age of the texts, as *Critical Text* does. While no major modern Bible translations rely solely on the *Majority Text*, versions like the World English Bible (WEB) and Modern English Version (MEV) are partially based on it.

Each tradition shapes modern translations, balancing historical evidence and textual scholarship to faithfully represent the New Testament.

The NIV Bible, which is one of the popular translations, like other translations based on Critical Text manuscripts, does not include Matthew 17:21 and not the *"fasting"* part of Mark 9:29. Therefore, depending on what manuscript tradition your New Testament was based on, you may not find Matthew 17:21 or only a part of Mark 9:29.

My point is that *the inclusion of "fasting" as a requirement for casting out certain kinds of demons does not appear in the earliest and most reliable manuscripts*, and it is generally not accepted as part of Jesus' original response when His disciples asked why they could not cast out the demon from the boy. The phrase appears in later medieval manuscripts—centuries after the earlier *Critical Text* manuscripts—and became widely known through 16th-century editions like the *Textus Receptus*. It is possible that Catholic scribes influenced by longstanding church traditions that emphasized fasting, particularly within monastic settings added the phrase. What is consistently found across all major manuscript traditions is that Jesus pointed to their lack of faith, which aligns with other Scriptures. To be clear and avoid bias, I should note that the New King James Version (NKJV), which I use daily, is based on the later *Textus Receptus* manuscript tradition and includes these disputed verses.

PART II. KNOW YOUR ENEMY

THE ROLE OF FASTING

To summarize, there is no evidence in the Bible that our prayers are in any way more powerful when we fast than when we do not fast. Apostle James says a righteous man or woman's prayer alone is powerful and effective—James 5:16. There is no evidence that fasting is a secret of great spiritual strength.

Jesus taught that fasting should be a private matter between you and God. He also said that *when*, *why*, or *how* often you fast is your personal choice. It is striking that none of the apostles *taught* about fasting, despite their emphasis on living right, knowing and trusting God's Word, and maintaining a vibrant prayer life.

Fasting is a spiritual practice paired with prayer to seek God's help, guidance or intervention. I believe fasting is another way to show our complete dependence on God for His support and blessings. Though I lack direct scriptural support, my personal experience tells me that fasting, when done properly, strengthens our prayers before God.

There are believers who do not live right but believe or have been led or taught to believe that through fasting they can resolve all their problems. However, the Bible says, "*Do not be deceived, God is not mocked; for whatever a man sows, that he will also reap*"—Galatians 6:7 NKJV. I previously referenced the story of King David fasting and praying for his son conceived through adultery with Bathsheba to live—1 Samuel chapter 11. God did not answer that prayer in spite of his fasting. We cannot force God's hand through our fasting or get Him to do for us what He would not do.

Fasting is, however, a powerful spiritual discipline that energizes and sharpens our inner being. It helps us tune out distractions and become more sensitive to the Holy Spirit. Revelation 1:10 says, "*I was in the Spirit on the Lord's Day*" referring to John's spiritual state when he received his visions. In the church, we generally believe that this phrase implies he was fasting, though Scripture does not explicitly say so. Regardless, fasting puts us in a posture to hear more clearly from God.

When we fast, our flesh weakens but our spirit becomes more alert. This is what Jesus meant in Mark 14:38 when He said, "*The spirit indeed is willing, but the flesh is weak*" (NKJV). In fasting, the cravings and distractions of our natural selves are subdued, while our spiritual senses become heightened.

Fasting also has physical benefits. I once read a business article that said many executives in Silicon Valley, the heart of America's technology industry, fast regularly for better health. If your goal is to lose weight, fasting may be a safer and more effective approach than relying on medications with side effects or supplements that may harm your body in other ways.

I have written this chapter about fasting to dispel the "myths" about fasting being a super or miracle weapon or a source of some secret power by which we can accomplish things or force God's hands. It is not. Jesus said, " . . . *you shall know the truth, and the truth shall make you free*" (John 8:32, NKJV). If we are to walk in victory, we must hold fast to the truth and practice only what is true.

Fasting strengthens our spirits, but it is not a secret of great strength for spiritual warfare. True strength for spiritual warfare comes from living righteously, having a deep knowledge of and faith in the Word of God, and maintaining an active prayer life. We must consistently practice these core fundamentals. They form the foundation for the next two chapters. In chapter eight, I will present the scriptural basis for how we release God's power through our words. Then, in chapter nine, I will explore practical ways to activate and release that power.

PART III

POWER IN YOUR MOUTH

Chapter 8

Power in Your Mouth

We have now reached the third part of this book, and I pray that God opens your spiritual eyes and ears to see and hear His message. Amen.

Some of you believe you need to do big things to beat the devil, but that is not true. You can have victory over him by knowing the right steps to take. You might think, or others might tell you, that fasting is the key to overcoming. That is not so. As we covered in chapter seven, fasting is not a spiritual weapon. God's ways are straightforward. Stick to what the Bible says, and you will always be on the right path. What does the Scripture say? Psalm 8:2.

> *Out of the mouth of babes and sucklings*
> *hast thou ordained strength because of thine enemies,*
> *that thou mightest still the enemy and the Avenger.*

The secret to your victory, freedom, and deliverance lies in the words you speak as the scripture says *"Out of the mouth . . . "* The power to silence the devil and defeat the enemy is in your mouth. When God's people do not know this, they chase after one church leader to another, when God has already given them the key.

Writing by the Holy Spirit, the Spirit of revelation, King David, the psalmist, declares that the power to silence the enemy in your life is in your words. It is not in fasting, but in your mouth. Your words carry the power to silence your enemies. If you know how to speak, you can tell the devil or any foe to be quiet about you.

Your victory and breakthrough are in your mouth, ready for you to speak them into reality. The devil may be running rampant in your life because you have not learned how to talk to him. Some might say it is not that easy, but this is not just my opinion—it is God's truth. Psalm 8:2 says God has ordained it that your words hold that power.

PRINCIPLE OF DOMINION

God has ordained power through our mouths to ensure our victory over the devil. We could never overcome the devil by our own strength, so God secured the victory for us through Jesus Christ and made it accessible through our spoken words. This is a principle of dominion by which even God Himself operates. Let me share some verses to illustrate this.

> *You will rule them with an iron scepter; you will dash them to pieces like pottery.*
> Psalm 2:9 (NIV)

> *The Lord will extend your Mighty scepter from Zion; You will rule in the midst of your enemies.*
> Psalm 110:2 (NIV)

Psalm 2:9 speaks of Jesus—the Anointed One—ruling over His enemies. Psalm 110:2 expresses the same idea but that Jesus is going to rule through Zion, which is the Church. You will notice that in both verses, the instrument of the ruling or dominion is the scepter. Of course, this is also true of earthly monarchs. A scepter is a symbolic rod or staff held by rulers, representing authority, sovereignty, and power. It is a symbol signifying royal or imperial power and governance. What then is the mighty or iron scepter to which the Psalm refer? We find the answer in Revelations 19:15 (NIV).

> *Out of his mouth comes a sharp sword with which to strike down the nations. He will rule them with an iron scepter . . .*

Here, Apostle John says that the Lord is going to strike down the nations with the sword of His mouth and by quoting Psalm 2:9, he indicates that the sharp sword is the *Iron Scepter*. We know that the sharp sword is the sword of the Spirit. Apostle Paul says, in Ephesians 6:17 that " . . . *the sword of the Spirit, which is the word of God."*

Jesus rules and reigns through the words He speaks, and God has set it up so we, too, can rule and take charge through our words. This is God's design—you cannot improve or add to it. Just do what God's Word says, not what anyone else tells you. I have learned that to get the results promised in God's Word, you must follow what it says—plain and simple. There is no shortcut. Do not act as if you know better than God.

For example, God's Word is clear: *"Give, and it will be given to you . . . "*—Luke 6:38. You cannot expect to receive if you do not give. Endless prayers or fasting will not twist God's arm or bribe Him. Just do what God says—do not think you know better than He does.

God's Word in your mouth is your iron scepter, your instrument of dominion. Whether you win or lose life's battles hinges on what you speak. The words you say when facing your enemy will either *secure your victory or register your defeat*. What you say will either lock in your victory or seal your defeat on the day of battle:

> When you are sick,
> When the enemy frightens you with negative thoughts of death or accident,
> When someone curses you,
> When you are confronted with witchcraft or sorcery,
> When your manager or supervisor at work threatens to fire you,
> When the enemy is trying to mess up the life of your children.

The Ten Spies

Poised at Canaan's border, the ten spies who brought back a negative report about the land spoke these shocking words: *" . . . We can't attack those people; they are stronger than we are."*—Numbers 13:31 NIV.
What is more, the people trusted their words. Because of this, they never stepped into the land flowing with milk and honey. Maybe saying or believing "I cannot" is why you have not reached your own "Canaan" in parts of your life—like your health, business, finances, or marriage.

What you claim you cannot do or become, you will never achieve or be until you change your confessions. You are what you say you are. If you believe and declare you are healed, healing will come. Quit thinking or saying you cannot overcome. The reason you have not won is not that you are unable—it is because you keep saying and believing you cannot. You are bound by your confessions. Change those negative confessions.

The ten spies claimed their enemies were stronger than they were. Your enemy only becomes stronger when you say so. Your words can either empower your foe against you or weaken them. Your words will either disarm your enemy or arm them. Your confessions either make your adversary mightier than you or make you mightier than them.

David versus Goliath

Your words carry great power. When you speak the right words on the day of battle, God will back you up, confirming everything you say. Take a look at what David said to Goliath:

> *This day the Lord will deliver you into my hand,*
> *and I will strike you and take your head from you.*
> *And this day I will give the carcasses of the camp of the Philistines*
> *to the birds of the air and the wild beasts of the earth, . . .*
> *Then all this assembly shall know that the Lord does not save with*
> *sword and spear . . .*
> 1 Samuel 17:46–47 NKJV

When you read the story carefully, you will notice that God fulfilled every word David spoke. David declared, "I will," and he did. You, too, can overcome your enemy. You have not been losing because your enemy is a Goliath—it is because you have either stayed silent or spoken the wrong words. Your confessions shape your reality. God will stand with you, but only if you speak the right things.

David said that God does not save by sword or spear. By what then does the Lord save? Romans 10:10 provides the answer.

> *For it is with your heart that you believe and are Justified,*
> *and it is with your mouth that you confess and are saved.*
> (NIV)

You became born again or saved by confessing your faith. In the same way, God will rescue you in the day of battle through your confessions. Do not be afraid to speak to your enemy, even if he is as daunting as Goliath is. David, a young man with no battle experience, took down the giant Goliath—a seasoned warrior who " . . . *has been a fighting man from his youth*"—by the power of his spoken words.

How did David do it? He knew a secret. He knew that God had ordained power through his mouth—power to silence the enemy and avenger.

Power in Your Mouth

We know this was the case because David wrote Psalm 8:2. It worked for David, it will work for you too if you believe it. Even if you consider yourself a *"babe or suckling,"* you can defeat that enemy.

God is faithful and will stand behind you, confirming every word you speak to your enemy. Do not hesitate to speak boldly and keep speaking. Your victory hinges on your confessions. God is listening, waiting to hear your words. There is power in your mouth. Release that power.

Chapter 9

Release the Power

IN THE PREVIOUS CHAPTER, we learned that the power to overcome our enemies lies in our words. Through our mouths, God has ordained strength to silence the Enemy and the Avenger. However, that power must be released, or our enemies will not be silenced. Therefore, we need to understand how to release this power. Let me share three ways to unleash that power.

CONFESS YOUR VICTORY

Confessing your victory means speaking words of faith. A confession of faith is either declaring God's Word directly or making bold statements rooted in it. Understand that any confession not grounded in God's Word is not true faith, as only His Word is the word of faith (Romans 10:8). You need to learn to speak to your enemy. Your victory depends on saying the right things. *When you speak the Word of God, you invite God into your situation. You get God on your side.* The Bible says in Mark 16:20

> *Then the disciples went out and preached everywhere,*
> *and the Lord worked with them*
> *and confirmed his word by the signs that accompanied it.*

Sometimes you may find yourself in a situation where it feels like God is not there. However, it could be that you are saying the wrong things. When you speak God's Word in the middle of your battles, He shows up—just like He did with the disciples—and He will confirm His Word. God does not back up just any words; He confirms what aligns with His Word. The same goes for what anyone else says—only His Word carries that confirmation.

If all you can remember in the day of battle is something your pastor or minister said, you might find yourself defeated. Some believers build their entire lives around the sayings of different ministers, but that is a risky way to live. There is no revelation or prophetic word greater than the Word of God itself. Get His Word into your heart—it is what you need most.

Let me show you three reasons why you need to learn to speak the Word of God and make confessions based on the Word.

1. *The Word of God is The Carrier of God's Power.* The Bible says that the Word is "the *word of his (God) power*"—Hebrews 1:3 (KJV) and "*where the word of a king is, There Is Power: and who may say unto him, what doest thou?*"—Ecclesiastes 8:4 (KJV). Remember, God created the world through His spoken words—He simply spoke, and everything came into existence. God's Word carries His power.

2. *The Word of God Commands Satan's Obedience.* Satan has no regard for your words or anyone else's. You cannot move him with human speech. However, the Word of God will move him—anytime, any day—because it is the Sword of the Spirit. In Matthew 4, our Lord Jesus shows us exactly how to resist and overcome the devil. Some people believe Jesus overcame simply because He fasted for 40 days and nights. While fasting may have played a part—helping to subdue His flesh and strengthen His spirit—it was not the source of victory. The real victory came through the Word of God. Jesus spoke the Word, and even though the devil resisted twice, he eventually gave way. The devil might push back in your own situation too, but hold on—he will give way in the end. The Word of God will move him. Your fasting alone will not move the devil. He is not afraid of your fasting, even if it lasts 40 days like it did with Jesus or Moses. As long as fasting is all you do, the devil remains unbothered—otherwise, he would not have tempted Jesus after His 40 days of fasting. *Your fasting will move God's hand if it is acceptable, but you need the Word of God to move the devil.* If fasting had power over the devil, Jesus would not have needed to speak the Word. Jesus spoke the Word and set an example for us to follow.

3. *The Word of God Gives You Access Into the Spiritual Realm.* As you know, the battle with the devil is a spiritual one. However, because we are flesh and blood, we need a way to connect with the spiritual

world. The Word of God provides that access. The Lord Jesus says, "... *The words that I speak to you are spirit, and they are life."*—John 6:63 NKJV. The Word of God is Spirit, giving us access to the spiritual realm where the outcomes of our physical lives are decided. It is in this spiritual place that we must first secure our victory before it appears in the physical world.

Stop Confessing Defeat

Another important aspect of confessions to understand is negative confessions. The devil thrives and rejoices when you speak negatively about yourself or others. He often sets up situations to tempt you into saying the wrong things. There is power in words, as Proverbs 18:21 declares:

> *The tongue has the power of life and death,*
> *and those who love it will eat its fruit.*
> (NIV)

Some people suffer due to their own confessions or because of what other people have said about them. Such is the case of Jabez in 1 Chronicles 4:9–10. His mother named him *Jabez*, meaning "sorrow," and sorrow followed him. He faced constant struggles and pain. He was always experiencing pain until God changed his situation.

Like Jabez, there are people who are suffering because of the things that have been spoken about them, sometimes even by those who love them. I suspect that Jabez's mother loved him but that there was a negative situation in her life at the time of his birth. As a result, she named him sorrow.

Another person who was given the wrong name was *Ichabod*, the grandson of Prophet Eli and son of Eli's son Phinehas. His mother died giving birth to him because she suddenly went into labor after she heard that her husband and Eli, her father-in-law had died and that the Philistines had captured the Ark of God. Therefore, she named her son "Ichabod" which means, "*The glory has departed from Israel*"—1 Samuel 4:19–22.

Benjamin, the son of Jacob was another person who was given the wrong name at birth. His mother Rachel had great difficulty giving birth to him and while she was passing away, she named him *Ben-Oni* that means "*son of my trouble*." However, Jacob knowing the power of having the right name because God had just changed his name to Israel changed the boy's name to Benjamin, which means "*son of my right hand*." Genesis 35:16–20.

In America and in the West generally, people's names do not mean or stand for anything because there is general ignorance of the significance and the power of names. God changed Abraham's name from Abram, which means, "*exalted father*" to Abraham because He said that Abraham would be the "*father of many nations*." He changed Jacob's name, which means "*supplanter*" to Israel.

The name you give your child could set the course of their lives and destiny. Give your child a meaningful name that reflects your hopes for their lives or what you believe will be God's purpose for their lives. Give your child a name that has a godly association and not a name like "*Delilah*." Jabez's name almost ruined his life until he prayed to God.

Sometimes people blame God for their misfortunes when the things someone else has spoken about them may have caused it. Jabez's mother was responsible for his misfortune.

You need to find out the reason for your afflictions. Stop blaming God. As parents, we must be careful about what we say to our children. You must refuse and nullify every negative thing anybody says about you. The more important thing however is what you say about yourself. The devil knows that there is power in your mouth and so it pleases him when you say negative things about yourself. In fact, the devil will try to manipulate you to say the wrong things.

This is why you must not make confessions based on your negative circumstances. No matter how bad your situation may be, choose to align your confessions with what the Word of God says. The Bible says, "*for we walk by faith not by sight*"—2 Corinthians 5:7 KJV. The devil will want you to say the wrong things but you must continue to confess the word of God. Your change will come. The word of God will create the change you want.

Control Your Tongue

What you say is crucial for your victory or defeat. *The life of a man or woman is governed and controlled by his or her words.* Apostle James says:

> *. . . if anyone can control his tongue,*
> *it proves that he has perfect control over himself in every other way*
> James 3:2 (TLB)

What James is pointing out is that if you can control your tongue, it shows you have self-control. In addition, in the same way, when you can control your tongue, you can also control your life. *If you control your confessions, you control the circumstances of your life.* Some people's lives are out of control because of the negative and reckless things they say.

Apostle James, in James 3:3 (NIV), says, *"When we put bits into the mouths of horses to make them obey us, we can turn the whole animal."* He is pointing out that a horse's mouth controls its direction. He also likens the tongue's power over our lives to a ship's rudder, stating, *"Or take ships as an example. Although they are so large and are driven by strong winds, they are steered by a very small rudder wherever the pilot wants to go"* (verse 4, NIV). A tiny rudder controls even massive ships.

Similarly, the devil knows he cannot control your life unless he controls your tongue. That is why he pushes you to speak the wrong words, so he can gain power over your life.

Some individuals have surrendered control of their lives to Satan through the words they speak. Then they wonder why the devil wreaks havoc in their circumstances. You can and should take charge of your life by controlling your tongue. Confessions hold immense power. Your healing, deliverance, or transformation may not come because of your negative confessions.

I remember an incident in my life many years ago. I was experiencing a physical pain and even though I was praying and confessing the relevant Bible promises, it persisted. Therefore, after some days, I asked the Lord why. The Lord told me to change my confessions. He made me understand that even though I was praying, I was still confessing that I was weak and that that was the reason for its persistence.

No matter how long or hard you pray if you do not align your confessions with the word of God, your prayers will not work. Moreover, this is the reason why even with prayers, the change you desire may not happen.

Get your confessions right. Be in charge of your life. God wants you to be. Do not let the devil control your life and circumstances because of your negative confessions. Remember Proverbs 18:21 (NIV) says, *"The tongue has the power of life and death, and those who love it will eat its fruit."* What you confess, will happen to you.

HIGH PRAISES OF GOD

It is noteworthy that certain Bible translations, such as the NIV, render the word translated as *strength* in the KJV version of Psalm 8:2 as *praise*.

Indeed, when Jesus referenced this verse during the Triumphal Entry in Matthew 21:16, He declared:

> . . . *Out of the mouth of babes and nursing infants You have perfected praise*

Thus, Jesus substituted the word *strength* with *praise*. As noted, the NIV translation of the verse also uses *praise* instead of *strength*.

Praise is one of the ways to release the power in your mouth. When you live a life of praise, God will silence many of your enemies without you even realizing it. Praise is one of the weapons of our warfare. Psalm 149:5–9 says:

> *Let the saints be joyful in glory; Let them sing aloud on their beds. Let the high praises of God be in their mouth, And a two-edged sword in their hand, To execute vengeance on the nations, And punishments on the peoples; To bind their kings with chains, And their nobles with fetters of iron; To execute on them the written judgment— This honor have all His saints . . .*

The first point to notice is that the Psalmist links praise with a double-edged sword, showing that praise is also a weapon of warfare. Our double-edged sword is the Word of God.

The second point it shows us is what praise and the Word of God can accomplish. Through praise and the Word:

- You can inflict vengeance on, and punish your enemies.
- You can bind them with fetters and shackles of iron.
- And, you can carry out the sentence written against them

There is a sentence written against the devil and his hosts, and you can execute that sentence through praise.

I began to understand that praise is a powerful weapon of warfare through a night experience I had many years ago when I was much younger. I had a frightening dream where some evil people were trying to harm me. I woke up shaken, and the fear grew stronger as I sensed a heavy demonic presence in the room. I considered waking up my brothers, who were also in the house, but I realized that would not solve the problem.

I understood that this was warfare—I had to stand my ground and win. I realized that asking my brothers to pray with me would only delay the battle because the real issue was the devil challenging my confidence in God and His Word. This was a personal test, and I knew I had to face it alone and overcome.

However, I was so afraid that I could not do anything—not even speak the Word. In the middle of that fear, the Lord spoke to me and told me to praise Him in songs. And, that is exactly what I did. I began to sing and kept singing. After over an hour of praise, the fear lifted because the demonic presence had vanished.

The Divine Presence

At the time, I did not fully understand what happened that night but I have since. I believe that as I began to sing praises, the presence of God—the Holy Spirit—came down and the demonic host had no choice but to leave.

Whenever you sing praises to God, the Holy Spirit comes down. The Holy Spirit is God's presence. 2 Corinthians 3:17 says, "*Now the Lord is the Spirit, and where the Spirit of the Lord is, there is freedom.*" (NIV). When Paul and Silas sang praises to God in Acts chapter 16, the Holy Spirit came down, there was an earthquake and

> *. . . at once all the prison doors flew open, and everybody's chains came loose*
> verse 26

Your chains will be broken, and every door—whether shut by human or spiritual enemies—will swing open. Learn to praise God during crises and times of impossibility. *The devil cannot stay where God's presence is revealed. God's presence is more powerful than the strongest presence of the devil.*

Do you remember the story of Saul and David in 1 Samuel 16:14–23? The Bible says that whenever David played his harp, the evil spirit would leave Saul. This is because whenever David played the harp, the Holy Spirit came down.

If you live a life of praise, you will walk in victory. Therefore, you must cultivate a habit of praising God if you want to live a victorious life. Psalm 50:23 says:

> *He who sacrifices thank offerings honors me,
> and he prepares the way
> so that I may show him the salvation of God*

You honor God every time you praise Him. Praise brings glory to God. When God is glorified, He responds. He will show you His salvation. By praising God, you give Him room to step into your situation—you create space for Him to move on your behalf.

In 2 Chronicles 20, we read how Ammon, Moab, and Edom teamed up to attack Judah. On the day of battle, King Jehoshaphat put singers praising God at the front of his army. The Bible says, *"As they began to sing and praise, the Lord set ambushes against the people of Ammon, Moab, and Mount Seir, who had come against Judah"* (verse 22, NKJV). God turned the enemy armies against each other, causing them to destroy themselves. Praise is a powerful weapon. When you praise God in your struggles, He will silence your enemies, set traps (ambushes) for them as He did for Jehoshaphat, and deliver you from their schemes. *If you make praising God a habit, God will be silencing your enemies without you even knowing they are there.*

PRAY AHEAD OF THE BATTLE

In Ephesians chapter 6, after Paul described the defensive and offensive parts of the armor of God, he continues in verse 18:

> *And pray in the spirit on all occasions*
> *with all kinds of prayers and requests.*
> *With this [the warfare] in mind, be alert*
> *and always keep on praying for all the saints*
> (NIV)

Paul was emphasizing the critical role of prayer in spiritual warfare. He starts by saying, *"And pray . . ."* in verse 18, indicating that even after putting on the full armor of God, prayer is essential. Moreover, you should pray not only when you feel like it, but *"on all occasions."*

This means you should pray whenever the chance arises—whether it is day or night, in private or in public, inside the church or anywhere else.

Whenever there is an opportunity to pray, Paul says, seize the opportunity, do not let it slip. He says, *"Be very careful, then, how you live—not as unwise but as wise, making the most of every opportunity because the days are evil."* Ephesians 5:16–16.

We must acknowledge that these truly are evil times. This is clear when we look at the rise in road accidents, plane crashes, armed robberies, and murders affecting our communities. We also see businesses and economies collapsing because of greed and corruption, along with widespread famine and starvation. All of these reflect the fallen state of a world under the devil's influence. When you observe the moral decline in society—the increasing divorce rates, pedophilia, homosexuality, and all the confusion around gender identity—it becomes obvious that the days are indeed evil.

The Bible clearly states there are only two genders—male and female—as seen in Genesis 1:27 (NKJV): "*So God created man in His own image; in the image of God He created him; male and female He created them.*" This truth is also evident in our biology, an undeniable reality despite the confusion of diversity, inclusiveness, and political correctness. Marriage, instituted by God as the foundation for family, is under intense demonic attack because it forms the bedrock of society and the raising of godly children.

The Days Are Evil

You must prepare in advance for the evil day, the day of spiritual warfare. Do not wait until the battle starts to pray, as you may not have time. The saying, "*In peacetime, prepare for war,*" comes from the wisdom of nations that train their armies, stockpile resources, and plan strategies long before conflict arises. Likewise, in spiritual warfare, you need to maintain an active and regular prayer life and pray ahead of the day of battle.

Seize every chance to pray now while you have time. Make the most of these moments. To be ready for spiritual battles, you need to pray long before the fight comes. Prayer is the key to preparation. Get into the habit of praying for your future, sending prayers ahead, so that on the day of battle, God will stand with you.

Praying ahead for yourself and your loved ones future is an incredibly powerful thing to do. God began to show me this very early in my Christian walk. Prayer gives us the power to begin to shape our future and determine what it will look like. This is not to say that we can pray out troubles and pain in life because these are a part of this life for believers and unbelievers alike. Jesus said " . . . *In this world you will have trouble. But take heart! I have overcome the world.*"- John 16:33 (NIV). However, we can begin to affect our future by making sure that God's grace, mercies and help are there when and if we need them.

Jesus prayed in the Garden of Gethsemane (Mark 14:32–42) before His arrest, torture, and crucifixion. He prayed for at least one hour, possibly three hours or more, if we estimate that He prayed for an hour each of the two additional times He withdrew, with some time passing between checking on His disciples. Through prayer, He gained the strength to face

His accusers, mockers, and torturers. In the Sermon on the Mount, He also instructed us to pray proactively, teaching us to ask God to deliver us from the evil one. This is praying ahead of the day of evil.

Do you have young children you hope will attend college someday? Begin praying now that God will guide them to the right college and help them select the appropriate major. Do you have teenagers you wish to see married one day? Start praying now that they will meet and choose the right spouse. Do you have adult children from whom you are anticipating grandchildren although they are not yet married? You can pray now that their children—your grandchildren—will be healthy, free from medical or mental health challenges, and will not fall into homosexuality or stray from the path of righteousness.

It is never too early to start praying these prayers. Sometimes, the devil targets our children and grandchildren because he cannot reach us directly. God sees the whole span of our lives and views us through the lens of generations. Long before Abraham had Isaac, God told him, *"I will make your offspring like the dust of the earth, so that if anyone could count the dust, then your offspring could be counted."* - Genesis 13:16 (NIV).

God was already seeing Abraham's generations to come. When we pray ahead, God is present at the battle before we arrive, standing before the devil to frustrate his plans. He will be there to secure the victory for us. Remember, the key to getting God ahead of the devil is to pray ahead.

As a teenager visiting my older brother, I narrowly escaped a life-threatening incident, spared only by Divine intervention. One of the two lights at the gate to the house had stopped coming on, so I decided to fix it. Noticing a disconnected wire, I planned to strip its insulation and re-connect it. Without a wire stripper or electrical scissors, and mistakenly assuming the light switch was off and that the circuit was dead, I used my teeth to strip the insulation. After reconnecting the wire, the light immediately turned on, revealing that the circuit was live the entire time. Reflecting on this, I recognize the foolishness of my actions, but I am grateful for God's protection who shielded me from potential electrocution by being ahead of the devil and me.

Praying on all occasions also means pray at all times: when you are walking or driving the street or road; even when you are bathing or doing laundry; when in your school or in your place of work; when traveling on air, land or sea; when in the restroom or in the kitchen cooking or doing chores, pray. Pray on all occasions. This is what Charlotte Elliott, the writer of the hymn "Christian, Seek Not Yet Repose" meant when she says:

> Principalities and powers,
> mustering their unseen array,
> wait for thy unguarded hours;
> 'watch and pray.

This is the reason why you should pray on all occasions. A good way to do this is to pray in tongues. You can pray in tongues anywhere under your breath without disturbing anyone or attracting attention. Even when you cannot concentrate, you can speak or pray in tongues.

Pray in Tongues

I first mentioned praying in tongues in chapter four and I am aware that there are churches and believers who believe that speaking or praying in tongues is past and is no longer for us. I will not try to change your mind except to say that it is still for us. The Bible is clear about this. Jesus Christ, the ultimate Authority on Divine Truth says in Matthews 16:17

> *And these signs will follow those who believe:*
> *In my name they will cast out demons;*
> *they will speak with new tongues . . .*
> (NKJV)

The speaking in new tongues that Jesus spoke of here was first fulfilled on the day of Pentecost when it says in Acts 2:4 "*And they were all filled with the Holy Spirit and began to speak with other tongues, as the spirit gave them utterance.*" Speaking in tongues is evidence of being filled with the Holy Spirit; it means speaking in another language—one that is not your native tongue. In Acts 2:7-11, we see the believers speaking in the language of other nations. Later on, in the same chapter, Apostle Peter said " . . . *you shall receive the gift of the Holy Spirit. For the promise is to you and to your children, and to all who are afar off, as many as the Lord our God will call*"—Acts 2:15.

If you are a believer and believe that the Lord has called you, then speaking in tongues is for you. However, if you think it is not your thing, I will not push. Let me just share a few points that might encourage you to think it over.

- In spiritual warfare, difficult situations sometimes call for longer prayers to break through. You may need to wrestle in prayer, like Jacob did in Genesis 32:24 (see chapter 10 for more) or as Jesus did in the Garden of Gethsemane. You can only pray so long in words you know, but praying in tongues helps you keep going. Apostle Paul said, "*I thank my God I speak with tongues more than you all*" (1 Corinthians 14:18, NKJV). In Gethsemane, Jesus had prayed for an hour when He checked on His disciples, saying to Peter, "*What! Could you not watch with Me one hour?*" (Matthew 26:40, NKJV). Can you pray for even thirty minutes or more? You should endeavor to pray at least 30 minutes daily. Praying in tongues makes that possible.

- In Romans 8:26, Apostle Paul writes, "*We do not know what we should pray for as we ought, but the Spirit Himself makes intercession*" (NKJV). When you are unsure what to pray or feel confused, praying in tongues is the best thing to do. The Holy Spirit prays through you and always knows the perfect prayers to offer to God.

- Praying in tongues is a particularly very good spiritual exercise. 1 Corinthians 14:4 (NKJV) says, "*He who speaks in a tongue edifies himself . . .*" When you pray in tongues, you energize your spirit. My personal Christian experience leads me to conclude that the regenerated human spirit is like the engine of a car. If a car sits unused—never driven or warmed up—the battery drains. Therefore, for your car to remain in top shape ready to go when you start it, you need to keep the battery from draining. Similarly, to keep your spirit strong and ready, you must actively nurture it to avoid 'running down'. Paul says, "*For if I pray in a tongue, my spirit prays . . .*"—1 Corinthians 14:14 (NKJV). When you pray in tongues, you exercise your spirit. If you want to remain in top shape spiritually, praying in tongues is one way to do it. Speaking in tongues warms up your spirit and keeps you in top spiritual health as warming your engine keeps your automobile in top mechanical health if you keep up with other maintenance. I speak in tongues every single day, often several times throughout the day.

- Lastly, praying in tongues is a secret weapon that confounds the devil and his forces because they cannot figure out what you are saying. Let me use an analogy from the Information Technology profession. In cybersecurity, especially cryptography, encryption protects the privacy and security of data and communications. There are two main types: symmetric and asymmetric encryption. In symmetric encryption, all participants share a single secret key. In asymmetric encryption, each person has a key pair—a public key they share for encrypting messages and a private key they keep secret for decrypting those messages—allowing secure communication by using each other's public keys. Praying in tongues is your private key to talk to God in a secret code that only He understands, locking out the devil and everyone else. When you pray in tongues, the Holy Spirit prays through you, and only God knows the mind of the Holy Spirit. It is the language of the Holy Spirit. Apostle Paul writes, *"He [God] who searches the hearts knows what the mind of the Spirit is, because He [the Holy Spirit] intercedes for the saints according to God's will"* (Romans 8:27, NKJV). Do you not want to connect with God like this?

Let me now share two more stories that show the amazing power of praying in tongues, building on my earlier account, in chapter four, of scaring off three dogs that tried to attack me at night by speaking in tongues.

When my son was around five, he developed a dangerously high fever one night—the kind that sends people to the emergency room. We were ready to rush him to the hospital if needed. Let me add that I firmly believe in faith healing, but I disagree with preachers who insist we must reject all medical treatments or even traditional home remedies. The Bible shows God Himself prescribing remedies. For example, the prophet Isaiah instructed King Hezekiah to apply a fig poultice to his boil for healing (Isaiah 38:21, NIV). Likewise, Apostle Paul advised Timothy to take a little wine for his frequent infirmities (1 Timothy 5:23, NIV). We did not have to rush him to emergency because I prayed over him, speaking in tongues, and God healed him almost instantly.

Another example of God healing through my praying in tongues was a few years ago when my brother-in-law and his family were visiting us. One day, his adopted son came down with a high fever, similar to the one my son had. I prayed over him in tongues, and God healed him swiftly and he made a quick recovery.

Matthew 16:17, which I mentioned earlier, shows that spiritual gifts are for believers. Speaking in tongues is one such gift the Lord gives to His people. You are still a believer even if you do not speak in tongues or feel it is not for you. However, I will tell you this—you are missing out on the power that comes from praying in tongues.

Release the Power

Jacob Wrestled God

Let me illustrate the role and power of prayer in spiritual warfare by the story of Jacob when he was preparing to meet his brother Esau in Genesis chapter 32. First, the Bible says in James 5:16

> ... *The prayer of a righteous man is powerful and effective.* (NIV)

> ... *The earnest prayer of a righteous man has great power and wonderful results.* (TLB)

> ... *The earnest (heartfelt, continued) prayer of a righteous man makes tremendous power available [dynamic in its working]."* (AMPC)

Know this: your prayers can unleash powerful, awesome strength to crush demonic forces. You can release amazing, life-changing results for you, your loved ones and others through the incredible power of prayer.

Jacob knew that he was going to pass through Esau's territory on his way back to their father. It appears that Rebecca, his mother, had already died at this time because the Bible did not say anything about her. The Bible recorded Deborah, Rebecca's nurse death in Genesis 35:8; Rachel, Jacob's wife death in verse 16–20; and Isaac's death later in verse 27–29 but did not say anything about Rebecca.

He also very well remembered what he had done to Esau. Therefore, he decided to send messages ahead to ask for Esau's favor. You see, Jacob was starting on a wrong note here. Instead of praying first so that God will be there for him at the point of meeting Esau, he chose to send messages to ask for favor first. The first thing you must do in any crisis or threat situation is pray.

This was the wrong step. Favor comes from God, and when you have favor with God, He will cause people to favor you. People will have no choice but to show you favor. Jacob should have prayed but he chose to send an appeal. This is not to say that apologizing for wrongdoing, asking for forgiveness or appealing for mercy is wrong. In fact, Jesus told us in Matthew 5:25 to make peace with our adversary (meaning anyone that we have wronged) before it becomes a legal case or we have to suffer the consequence. We should do this when we have the opportunity. However, the first thing we must do is to pray.

As soon as Esau heard the message, he mustered 400 men and started out to meet Jacob. The Bible did not explicitly say they were armed but given the time and Esau's hatred of Jacob, I believe they were armed. In military terms, 400-armed men is the size of 2–3 companies of soldiers depending on the country. I want you to understand that this was not a welcome party. It was like King David, enraged because Nabal had spurned and reviled them, led 400 of his armed men to go attack him and his family—1 Samuel 25:13. Esau was also coming to exact his revenge. You will remember that he previously vowed to kill Jacob—Genesis 27:41. If this was a welcome party, he would not need that many armed men and there would have been women in the company. Notice also that Esau did not respond to any of the messages Jacob had sent him.

Jacob understood this, which is why when he received the news, he became afraid, panicked and did what any fearful person would do. He resorted to the arm of the flesh, to merely human actions. He divided his people and flock into two, thinking (wishfulness) that if Esau attacked one group, the other group would be able to escape. He was willing to sacrifice one group for the safety of the other. It is a desperate person that would do this kind of thing.

Depend On the Holy Spirit

The Bible says " . . . *for by strength shall no man prevail.*"—1 Samuel 2:9 (KJV). We cannot win on the day of battle by wishful thinking or human tactics. Our enemy is too crafty for that. We need spiritual operational and tactical strategies, inspired by the Holy Spirit, to achieve victory. Mere wishful thinking will not suffice. We must pray. The outcome is determined in the place of prayer, on the battlefield of intercession. Jacob's tactics alone would have failed; Esau would have attacked both groups.

You must not panic on the day of battle because you will not win by panicking. Instead, you must pray instead of panic. In addition, if you do not want to panic on the evil day, you must learn to pray now and ahead of the day of battle.

In verse 9–12, Jacob decided to pray. However, his prayer was ineffective. You will not win on the day of battle by praying his kind of prayer. It was a prayer, prayed from fear and not from faith. It is the prayer of faith that saves—James 5:15 (KJV). I know that it was a prayer of fear because immediately after, in verses 13–21, he resorted to another human tactic.

He sent gifts in five groups to buy Esau's favor. The Bible says " . . . for he thought, *'I will pacify him with these gifts I am sending ahead . . . "*—verse 20. Another wishful thinking.

You see, you do not pacify your enemy; you prevail over him or her. This is a principle of spiritual warfare. You cannot appease the devil. Demonic forces will not and can never be appeased. You have to subdue them.

I want you to see something else. Jacob was ignorant of who his real enemy was. All this time, he saw Esau as his real enemy but the real enemy was the devil.

As soon as Jacob's message got to Esau, the demonic spirits of revenge and murder went to work. They reminded Esau of what Jacob did, more than 20 years ago, stealing his blessings. This caused the suppressed feelings to revive. The demons activated the desire for revenge latent within Esau and convinced him to murder his brother and possibly the whole family. All this time, Jacob was focused on Esau. He was not seeing the real enemy behind Esau. As a result, he was focusing all his efforts on appeasing Esau.

Develop Spiritual Perception

Apostle Paul says "*So from now on we regard no one from a worldly point of view . . .* " 2 Cor. 5:16 (NIV). You must learn to interpret every human action, especially in conflict situations, from the spiritual perspective. Many times, people do not act or speak of their own natural accord; spiritual forces influence them.

The battles of life (good or bad) are arranged in the spiritual world by spiritual forces. Therefore, for you to prevail in the physical, you must first prevail in the spiritual. *In the battles of life, the person who controls the spiritual wins*. If you must win, you must control the spiritual because the spiritual controls the physical. Again, this is a principle of spiritual warfare.

There is this story of Apostle Paul and a girl who had a spirit of divination in Acts 16:16-18. The Bible says this girl followed Paul and his companions doing "public relations" for them. Some ministers would have fallen for this but not Paul. In these days, when ministry for many is solely an opportunity for self-promotion and enrichment, many would certainly have fallen for the girl's antics. Apostle Paul says, "*For everyone looks out for his own interest, not those of Jesus Christ*"—Philippians 2:21 (NIV).

She kept this up for many days and Paul put up with it for those days. However, when he had become sufficiently troubled, he cast out the spirit that was influencing her. I want you to know that Paul could have reacted physically but he would have failed and might even have caused trouble for himself and his group. We know that this would have happened because, remember, the owners of this girl later brought law enforcement action against Paul and Silas (verse 19).

The girl would not have kept quiet if Paul had merely shouted at her because she was being influenced by demons. Moreover, if Paul had tried physically to restrain her, it could have led to some altercation. In fact, it is possible that the goal of the spirit at work in the girl was to provoke Paul to anger. Nevertheless, Paul read the situation correctly. He regarded her action not from a worldly point of view but from a spiritual one.

Therefore, he decided to control the physical from the spiritual. He cast out the spirit. As soon as he did that, the girl stopped. The way to stop your physical enemy is to stop the spiritual enemy.

You must not be foolish to fight your enemies physically. There is a spiritual dimension to life. The spiritual controls the physical. *When you control the spiritual, you automatically control the physical.* As soon as Paul controlled the spiritual, he controlled the physical.

Many years ago, a close Christian friend of mine had a very serious disagreement with his fiancée, so she decided to end their relationship. He had done everything to make amends but she refused to reconcile. He came to me very distraught over it. I immediately knew that the devil was at work and that we needed to control the spiritual. We went into battle praying in tongues and rebuking the demonic forces working behind the scenes. After we had prayed for a short time, the Holy Spirit told me to tell him to go back and speak to her again and that she would take him back. I was so sure of this that I thought within myself that if he were to come back to say she is still refusing to reconcile, I will tell him to go back again. However, he came back saying that she had accepted his apologies and that they were back together. They got married shortly after. This is the power of controlling the physical from the spiritual.

Now, let us go back to Jacob. He was ignorant of this spiritual dimension to the battles of life but God was not. God knew that all those things he was doing would accomplish nothing. He knew that what he should do was to pray and God wanted to bring him to the place of prayer, the battlefield of prayer.

In verses 22 to 23, Jacob sent his family and possessions across the brook and he was left alone. The Bible did not indicate what Jacob's intentions were or that he was planning to pray but God brought him to the place of prayer. God, sometimes, does this, inviting you to pray or bringing you to the place of prayer. Make sure to not ignore it. Verse 24 says,

> *So Jacob was left alone, and a man wrestled with him till daybreak."*
> (NIV)

The man who wrestled with Jacob was an angel representing God. This *"man"* initiated the wrestling. Therefore, it means God initiated the praying. Wrestling in this story is for us, as believers, an analogy for praying. Paul said of Epaphras, a Colossian believer " . . . *He is always wrestling in prayer for you . . .* " Colossians 4:12.

Jacob failed to discern that demonic influences were driving his brother Esau's actions. Rather than seeking God through prayer, he turned to appeasement and human strategies. *As believers, we must learn to distinguish whether individuals we encounter, particularly in conflicts, are acting independently or under demonic influence.* Prayer is a vital spiritual activity to engage divine supernatural forces and to triumph over demonic opposition.

Be Sensitive to the Spirit

We need to stay tuned in and sensitive to the Holy Spirit, ready to follow His nudges. Sometimes, He might stir you awake at night to pray, even when you are not in the mood or feel like it. This could show up as a heavy feeling, worry, or anxiety in your heart, or a clear urge to pray about something affecting you or someone else. Always respond to that call.

The Holy Spirit might be prompting you to pray because an enemy is near or the devil is setting traps He wants you to destroy through prayer. You can pray in tongues, even if you are unsure what to pray about. To those who think speaking in tongues is not for them: you are missing out on its blessings and power to overcome. Apostle Paul says in Romans 8:26–27:

> *In the same way, the Spirit helps us in our weakness. We do not know what we ought to pray for, but the Spirit himself intercedes for us through wordless groans. And he who searches our hearts knows the mind of the Spirit, because the Spirit intercedes for God's people in accordance with the will of God.* (NIV)

Speaking in tongues is wordless praying (or *groans* depending on the intensity). When we speak in tongues, the Holy Spirit is praying through us and for us.

There are countless testimonies of wonderful results accomplished by the people of God when they responded to the Holy Spirit prompts to pray. God has averted accidents, deaths, or disasters because someone responded to His call to pray.

Some years ago, a pregnant coworker, expecting her second child, was nearing delivery. One night, God showed me in a dream that she would die during childbirth. I immediately began praying in tongues for her. Later, I learned that the delivery was very difficult, but God spared her life. Many women have died from difficult deliveries. Through my prayers, God saved her. He has used my prayers many times to avert tragedies for others, and He wants to use your prayers too.

Once, I was driving home from work when I had this strong foreboding of danger ahead. Over the years, I have had the Holy Spirit prompt me in this way so I knew what it meant and what to do. Therefore, I said the name of Jesus a couple of times and spoke in tongues. By the way, just saying the name of Jesus when you are afraid or anxious is an incredibly powerful thing to do. The name of Jesus releases the power of God.

At an intersection, I made a left turn onto a road where the landscape obscures oncoming traffic. Immediately, I noticed a driver getting out of the opposite lane into mine and nearly colliding with me. By quickly applying my brakes, I avoided a certain accident. Reflecting on this narrow escape, I know that this outcome and deliverance is due to me previously responding to the prompting of the Holy Spirit.

You need to respond too. Your life or the life of your loved one—a brother or sister or friend—may depend on it. It was because Abraham prayed that Lot and his family were saved. They could have been destroyed if Abraham had not responded to God's call or invitation to pray—Genesis 18:20–33.

Decide the Outcome

Continuing with the story of Jacob, the outcome described in Genesis 33:4 was decided in the place of prayer. The Angel said to Jacob:

> . . . *you have struggled with God and with humans and have overcome.*
> Gen 32:28 (NIV)

"*God*," in that statement, represents the spiritual dimension and "*humans*" represents the physical dimension. In addition, more specifically, the "*humans*" in this story is Esau and his 400-armed men. You need to prevail in the spiritual first before you can prevail in the physical. Because he prevailed with God in prayers, he prevailed against the demonic forces and the physical forces—Esau and his 400-armed men. The Bible says in Genesis 33:4 (NIV):

> *"But Esau ran to meet Jacob and embraced him; he threw his arms around his neck and kissed him. And they wept."*

That outcome was brought about through the power of prayer. It worked for Jacob, and it will work for you. We have God's Word as our assurance. In the final chapter, I will highlight the reasons you may lose or are losing your battles, drawing insights from this story of Jacob's encounter with his brother Esau.

Chapter 10

Why You Lost the Battle

As I conclude the exposition of Psalm 8:2, I will highlight five key reasons, drawn from Jacob's story in Genesis 32, why you may lose in the day of battle. While some of these reasons have been touched on earlier, this chapter places them in clear context, offering a detailed discussion to position you for victory.

THE FEAR FACTOR

When Jacob heard the news that Esau was coming with 400-armed men, he was afraid and distressed—Genesis 32 verse 7. If you surrender or give in to fear in the day of battle, you will lose. The devil will attempt to scare and to make you afraid but you should not be for these reasons:

1. *Fear will drive your actions, often leading you astray from doing what is right.* When gripped by fear, King Saul offered a sacrifice reserved for priests, usurping Prophet Samuel's role, as described in 1 Samuel 13. Similarly, fear drove Prophet Elijah to flee into the desert from Jezebel, as recounted in 1 Kings 19. When fear takes hold, it clouds judgment, making it difficult to act in faith and righteousness. Apostle Paul says, *"For God has not given us a spirit of fear, but of power and of love and of a sound mind."* 2 Timothy 1:7. Notice that it says *"sound mind."* Fear is the enemy of a sound, rational mind. Paul also, in 2 Corinthians 5:7 reminds us, *" . . . we walk by faith, not by sight."* Fear also led Jacob to divide his family and possessions into two groups, hoping to save

one if Esau attacked the other—a flawed and fear-driven plan (Genesis 32). Faith, not fear, empowers you to make godly decisions.

2. *Fear signals an acknowledgment of your enemy's superiority*, effectively conceding defeat. However, you can stand fearless when you recognize that the greater One is with you, as affirmed in 2 Chronicles 32:7–8. King Hezekiah, facing the Assyrian king's threat, reassured his people, "*. . . for there is a greater power with us than with him.*" If you attribute superiority to your adversary, you limit God's ability to act on your behalf. *God will be to you what you make Him.* God's power in your life reflects the faith you place in Him.

3. *Fear will shape your confessions, undermining the victory.* As previously discussed, your victory hinges on your confessions. Gripped by fear, ten of the twelve spies sent by Moses to scout Canaan declared in Numbers 13:31 that they could not defeat the Canaanites, claiming their enemies were stronger. Their fearful confessions reflected unbelief, displeasing God, who ultimately judged them, and they perished in the wilderness. Your confessions of faith are critical to prevailing in spiritual battles.

4. *Fear will paralyze you, hindering your ability to fight.* As long as fear grips you, engaging in battle becomes unlikely, yet fighting is essential for victory. The Bible asks us to *"fight the good fight of faith"* (1 Timothy 6:12, NKJV), a battle deemed good because God has already secured your victory. The key to winning this fight is solely your faith; all else is secondary. Faith in God and His promises unlocks victory. As Apostle John declares in 1 John 5:4, "*. . . this is the victory that has overcome the world—our faith.*" Faith is your victory. Until Gideon conquered his fear of the Midianites, he could not engage them in battle (Judges 7). God's promise of victory was contingent on Gideon's willingness to fight. Likewise, you must fight to claim your victory. Know this: you have no reason to fear the devil or any enemy, whether spiritual or physical because *the enemy you fear, fears you.* This truth liberated Gideon from his fears. He learned that the Midianites, despite their superior numbers and weapons, were terrified of him (Judges 7:13–15). If you embrace this knowledge, you can fearlessly confront your adversaries and secure the victory God has promised. This revelation, that the enemy you are afraid of is in fact, afraid of you, also strengthened and emboldened the two spies Joshua sent to

Jericho (Joshua 2). Rahab, a local harlot, told them that after hearing of the Israelites' victory over the Amorite kings, Sihon and Og, "*... our hearts melted, and no one had any courage left because of you, for the Lord your God is God in heaven above and on earth below.*" The people of Jericho, gripped by fear, locked themselves in their city. When you embrace this truth, you will cast aside all fear of demons and their human agents. The devil fears you; you may just not realize it. How do I know? Because the devil trembled before Jesus during His earthly ministry, with demons screaming, shouting, and pleading in His presence (e.g., Mark 5:7). This applies to you because Jesus dwells in you. As 1 John 4:4 declares, "*... He who is in you is greater than he who is in the world*" (NKJV). With God on your side, you have no reason to fear the devil. Embrace this truth, and it will liberate you from fear, empowering you to walk boldly in victory.

You will never win if you always respond in fear and by only human actions in the day of battle or conflicts. This means that you responded only emotionally and not spiritually. What do you do when faced with opposition? Do you pray and remember the Word of God? Isaiah says:

> *Since ancient times no one has heard, no ear has perceived,*
> *no eye has seen any God besides you, who acts on behalf of those*
> *who wait for him.*
> *You come to the help of those who gladly do right, who remember*
> *your ways.*
> Isaiah 64:4–5 (NIV)

The times of conflicts and adversity is not the time to panic and act in desperation. If you want God to act for you, you must learn to wait on Him and remember His ways revealed in the Word of God—the Bible.

Remember also that humans are not your real enemies. Jacob was ignorant of his real enemy. Therefore, he was acting to frustrate Esau's designs. You should know that the battle is beyond the human agents. They are not your primary targets.

Do not forget that there is a spiritual dimension to life and conflicts. You must fight from this level if you want to win. *If you control the spiritual, you control the physical.* Your victory has to be determined in the spiritual realm. You must first realize your victory in the spiritual realm.

THE WRONG PRAYER

I previously said that Jacob's prayer in Genesis 32:9-12 was not very effective. The first reason is that it is a prayer of fear. The second reason is that it was the wrong prayer.

The Bible says *"And pray in the spirit on all occasions with all kinds of prayers and requests"*—Ephesians 6:18 (NIV). There are kinds of prayers, and the occasion determines the kind of prayer that you pray. Therefore, you must be able to read the occasion correctly to know the right prayer to pray.

For example, if you pray a prayer of *petition* when you should pray that of *thanksgiving*, it will be inappropriate and consequently ineffective. Jacob was praying a prayer of supplication or petition when he should be praying a warfare prayer or spiritual warfare prayer.

He was crying to God instead of addressing the demonic forces behind Esau. As I said before in a previous chapter, this was likely because he did not know who the real enemy was. On the day of battle or hostilities, you do not pray a prayer of *supplication* but a prayer of warfare. You do not cry to God but speak to the devil by wielding your God given authority.

In Exodus 14, as Moses and the Israelites faced the Red Sea with the Egyptian army closing in, the people panicked, and in typical fashion, confessed fear instead of faith. Moses, however, stayed calm, knowing this was part of God's plan. God had told him in verse 4 that He would harden Pharaoh's heart, prompting the pursuit. However, Moses did something God did not expect him to do. Instead of acting, he pleaded with and petitioned God in verses 13-14. God responded, " . . . *Why are you crying out to Me?*" (verse 15). The *"you"* in the Hebrew is a singular so God was speaking to Moses personally and not to the people who were frightened out of their minds and confessing their worst fears. Then, God instructed him to stretch out his staff over the Red Sea to part it, calling him to use the authority God had given him.

The rod or staff symbolized God's authority and power. When God told Moses to stretch it over the Red Sea, He was telling him to use that authority. This is also, what we must do in the day of battle. Instead of pleading with God, we must release God's power boldly against the enemy through warfare prayer.

Please understand—I am not saying there is no place for praying to God in the midst of battle. However, if you do not speak to the devil, you risk losing the fight. You must confront him in some way—whether through your confessions, prayers, or praise. Remember, the power to overcome your enemy is in your mouth. You must not stay silent on the day of battle. Even if you are afraid, speak to the devil anyway. In addition, make sure you are saying the right things, because your victory depends on it.

Perhaps, you have been speaking to your enemy and it seems that they will never give way. Do not be discouraged. Keep speaking; it will not be long before they give way. The word of God will move the devil anytime, any day. Remember that it was only after the third attempt that Satan left Jesus during the temptation in the wilderness. The devil cannot resist for long. Your words are weakening the demonic forces. Therefore, keep speaking. The testimony of Scripture in Revelations 12:11 is:

> *And they overcame him by the blood of the Lamb,*
> *and by the word of their testimony;*
> *and they loved not their lives unto the death.*
> (KJV)

This Scripture is the declaration of victory in the war between Archangel Michael with his angels and the Dragon (the devil) with his angels (demons) in verse 7. The Dragon and his angels did not prevail despite their bold and determined resistance.

In the same way, the devil will not prevail in your situation as long as you maintain your testimony, your faith confessions based on scriptures. You will wear him out if you persist with your testimony based on the Word of God. In the time of battle, you should not be afraid to speak to the demonic forces.

David would have lost the battle against Goliath in 1 Samuel 17 if he had kept quiet. The things that Goliath spoke against him would have happened. The Bible says he cursed David by his gods. What Goliath was doing was enlisting supernatural help. Let me unpack this.

Goliath was well aware of the power of the God of Israel. Growing up, he would have heard of God parting the Red sea through the hand of Moses, God destroying the Canaanites under the leadership of Joshua, etc. Therefore, he rightly understood that there is a spiritual dimension to conflicts. In fact, the Philistines were generally aware of the might and acts of the God of Israel. This was why when the Israelites brought the Ark of God into their camp during their battle with them in the time of Prophet Eli, the Bible says that the Philistines were greatly afraid and said:

> '... God [the God of Israel] has come into the camp!'
> And they said, 'Woe to us!
> For such a thing has never happened before. Woe to us!
> Who will deliver us from the hand of these mighty gods?
> These are the gods who struck the Egyptians
> with all the plagues in the wilderness'
> 1 Samuel 4:7–8 (NKJV)

Goliath knew all these, which was why he cursed David by his gods. By doing that, he was enlisting the help of his own gods; he was engaging the supernatural to help him defeat David. In fact, ancient peoples, as sometimes depicted in classical literature, generally seem to understand that they need the help of their gods or the supernatural to prevail in wars.

I do not endorse, in any way, the mythologies of classical literature, for example, like the Iliad, the epic that told the story of the Trojan War. In the story Homer, the writer, narrated how some of the Greek gods fought alongside the human combatants. I do not believe or accept the information in these literatures but I make mention of this only to the extent that these literatures convey the understanding that there is a supernatural world which indeed exists but not necessarily as it is described in the stories.

The idea of a supernatural world is not by any means original to classical or ancient literatures. The Bible is replete with stories that convey to us the existence of the supernatural, usually of the Divine. It is sad and unfortunate in modern times and in our generation that many people are ignorant of this because they have chosen to believe solely in science, which cannot prove or disprove the supernatural. There is a supernatural realm, both divine and demonic. In addition, it is not necessarily the supernatural often depicted in horror, or the so-called science fiction (sci-fi) movies.

Goliath knew this and initially despised David when he saw him approaching him. Then he cursed David by his gods saying, "... *Come to me, and I will give your flesh to the birds of the air and the beasts of the field!*"—verse 44 (NKJV). Although Goliath despised David, he also feared him because of David's God. This was why he enlisted the help of his own gods. *The enemy you fear, fears you.* Why? Because of your God who is God of gods, King of kings, and Lord of lords. David, too, also understood that he needed to enlist God's help and engage the supernatural. Therefore, he also responded to Goliath by saying in verses 46–47:

> *This day the Lord will deliver you into my hand,*
> *and I will strike you and take your head from you.*
> *And this day I will give the carcasses of the camp of the Philistines*
> *to the birds of the air and the wild beasts of the earth,*
> *that all the earth may know that there is a God in Israel.*
> *Then all this assembly shall know that the Lord does not save with*
> *sword and spear;*
> *for the battle is the Lord's, and He will give you into our hands.*
> (NKJV)

Every word that David spoke to Goliath happened. He indeed defeated and cut off the head of Goliath, and the Philistines army was defeated in battle that day. This is why you must say the right prayers on the day of battle.

FAILURE TO REBUKE

I was once in a prayer meeting where the Christian Brother who was leading the meeting asked us to pray that God should rebuke the devil for us. Indeed God can rebuke the devil for us but we can do it too and He wants us to. This was why Jesus gave us His authority:

> *Behold, I give you the authority to trample on serpents and*
> *scorpions,*
> *and over all the power of the enemy,*
> *and nothing shall by any means hurt you.*
> Luke 10:19 (NKJV)

Every Word of God is completely trustworthy—if you believe it, it will work for you. The devil does have real power, as Jesus stated in Luke 10:19, calling it *"the power of the enemy."* Do not ever doubt this. One clear example is Simon the Sorcerer in Acts 8, who used demonic power to astonish and captivate the entire Samaritan community for a long time. His was true sorcery, not the tricks or sleight of hand of today's so-called magicians.

You need to know that God's power is far greater than the devil's. Apostle Paul describes it as *"His incomparably great power"* (Ephesians 1:19, NIV). Do not ever doubt this as well—it is real and true. God has placed this power in our hands. If you are a born again believer who trusts all of God's Word, this power is yours. It is available only to those who believe. This power surpasses every power of the enemy.

The Lord has given us power to rebuke and overcome the enemy (the devil) and his demonic hosts. The Lord may rebuke the devil for us as He did in Zechariah 4 when Satan opposed or accused Joshua, the High Priest. The Lord says:

> *And the Lord said to Satan, 'The Lord rebuke you, Satan!*
> *The Lord who has chosen Jerusalem rebuke you!*
> *Is this not a brand plucked from the fire?'*
> *- verse 2 (NKJV)*

The Lord gave us authority to confront and rebuke the devil but there are those who say that it is incorrect for believers to rebuke the devil. They cite Jude 1:9 as evidence for this. However, what does the verse say?

> *Yet Michael the archangel, in contending with the devil,*
> *when he disputed about the body of Moses,*
> *dared not bring against him a reviling accusation,*
> *but said, 'The Lord rebuke you!'*

First, Jude said this in the context of false believers disrespecting and not submitting to church authorities—verse 8. I believe the point that Jude was making here is that even Archangel Michael respected Satan by not reviling him. Perhaps, because Archangel Michael was mindful of the fact that Satan was previously a fellow Archangel, when he was Lucifer, before his fall. Jude's point is that true believers need to respect church authorities and leadership. Apostle Peter wrote something similar in 2 Peter 2:10–11.

Second, this is not evidence that believers cannot or should not rebuke the devil because Archangel Michael did rebuke the devil except that he says *'The Lord rebuke you!'*." Meaning that he did rebuke the devil but in the name of the Lord and not in his own name. This is also, what we do as believers when we rebuke the devil.

Now that we have established that believers have the authority to rebuke the devil and demons, let us look at what rebuking a demonic entity actually means. The words "rebuke" or "rebuked" show up often in the Bible, both in the Old and New Testaments, with three main meanings. First, they are used to call out people or reprimand them for their sins. Second, they condemn or denounce unbelief or refusal to repent, like when Jesus scolded cities such as Capernaum and Bethsaida in Matthew 11:20–24 for refusing to repent in spite of His miracles. Third, they mean stopping or rejecting something harmful, as when Peter rebuked Jesus, insisting He would not die (Matthew 16:22). This third meaning—rejecting, or putting a stop, to evil—is what we are focusing on. I will share three examples from the Gospels of Mark and Luke to make this clear.

In Luke 4:39, Jesus rebuked the fever afflicting Peter's mother-in-law and it left her instantly, allowing her to rise and serve them. This was a case of immediate healing, though not all healings happen this quickly. In addition, the wording hints that a demon might have caused the fever. Some illnesses, like the one affecting the twelve-year-old boy I will discuss shortly, are indeed caused by demons.

We see Jesus address a demon possessed man in the synagogue in Luke 4:31–35. He rebuked and commanded the unclean spirit by saying *" . . . Be quiet, and come out of him!"* Then, the Bible says, the demon *" . . . threw the man down before them all and came out without injuring him"* (verse 35—NIV). This man was being destroyed from within, likely headed toward a fate like the Gadarenes demoniac, but Jesus stopped the devil's destructive work in its tracks.

Finally, Jesus rebuked the demonic spirit that was responsible for the epilepsy of the young boy in Mark 9:14–27. He cast out the demon and healed the boy. This was a boy that the devil was determined to destroy and had attempted many times to destroy. The Bible says in verse 25, that Jesus *" . . . rebuked the unclean spirit . . . "* by saying the following

> *Deaf and dumb spirit, I command you,*
> *come out of him and enter him no more!*

By this encounter, Jesus shows us what it means to rebuke the devil. By commanding the demon harming the boy to leave his body, He halted the devil's destructive work (Mark 9:25). Therefore, to rebuke the devil is to command him boldly to cease his attacks and schemes against us.

To rebuke the devil or demons is to reject, contradict or block something that would otherwise be harmful to us. We do this by speaking words or testimonies made based on the Word of God. Sometimes, it may not be something that is spoken but a negative thought that Satan plants in our mind or heart. That negative thought represents a *devil's attack plan*; it could be against our loved ones or us. We counter it by saying something positive or proclaiming a different outcome as David did against Goliath's curses. We can also stop ongoing harm as Jesus did when He commanded the demon to leave the boy's body—Mark 9:25. When we do not do this, we fail to engage or enlist divine or God's supernatural forces on our side as David did when he faced Goliath.

Let me explain why you must never ignore negative words spoken to you or negative thoughts planted by the devil. Sometimes, it could be a dream that shows something bad happening to you or a loved one. First, it reveals the *devil's attack plan*; second, they can come true if you do not counter them. In the book of Esther, Haman tricked the king into signing a decree to wipe out the Jews. After Haman's plot was stopped, Queen Esther begged the king to cancel the decree in Esther 8:3–6. However, the king said a decree signed with his ring could not be revoked based on Persian and Median law. Instead, he told her to write a new decree letting the Jews defend themselves.

Similarly, the devil will not back off his *attack plan*, so you must use the power of Jesus' name to stop it. As the Jews had to fight back on the day set for their destruction, you also need to stand up and fight, you need to rebuke or reject every demonic scheme. Do not ignore it, or it will come true.

Some say that it is only the Lord who can command demonic spirits and that believers cannot. Wrong! The seventy disciples commanded and cast out demons in Luke 10 when they said *"Lord, even the demons are subject to us in Your name."*—verse 17. *The enemy you fear, fears you.* Apostle Paul cast the demonic spirit of divination out of the slave girl in Acts 16:18. The other apostles did the same thing. Finally, Jesus gave us the authority to do this in Mark 16:17 when He says:

> *And these signs will follow those who believe:*
> *In My name they will cast out demons . . .*

We can command or cast out demons in the name of the Lord. If you are a believer, you can do this. The Lord has given us the authority and power to command the devil and demons and stop their attacks against us. In addition, the Lord has given us His angels to assist us to do this. Hebrews 1:14, speaking of Angels, says, *"Are they not all ministering spirits sent forth to minister for those who will inherit salvation?"* (NKJV).

Returning to Jacob's story, he lacked the understanding and grace available to us New Testament believers. In Genesis 32:9–12, he prayed a prayer of supplication, asking God in verse 11 to save him from Esau—a valid prayer under the Old Testament covenant, as the Lord indeed saves. Old Testament people do not have the authority to speak to demons. However, as New Testament believers, Jesus has given us this authority. While it is okay to pray a prayer of supplication when facing an adversary, God has empowered us to address the demonic forces behind human opposition. He has given us the authority to rebuke, command, and silence our enemies. He wants us to do this and He has given us the authority to do it.

If the devil is attacking your marriage, children, school, finances, business, work, health, or any area of your life, stand firm in the authority God has given you. Rebuke, command, and silence the enemy. Do not just cry and beg God to act for you—He wants you to use the power He has put in your hands. While God may intervene directly, He has primarily chosen you as His instrument to defeat the devil's schemes. Remember, *"Out of the mouth of babes and sucklings, you have ordained strength . . . "*—Psalm 8:2. Believers are God's *babes and sucklings* and there is power in your mouth.

FAILURE TO CONFRONT

In spiritual warfare, one key principle is clear: you cannot appease your enemy. The devil and his demonic forces will not be satisfied, no matter what you offer. Short of abandoning your faith and loyalty to God, there is no way to please the devil. Compromise was what the devil asked of our Lord Jesus when he offered all the world's kingdoms in exchange for worship, but Jesus firmly rejected him—and you must do the same. Compromising your faith will only lead to defeat. To win, you must stand firm and overcome these forces. Unlike earthly battles, spiritual warfare allows no truce, ceasefire, or neutral ground.

In Genesis 32:13-20, Jacob attempts to appease Esau. As I mentioned before, Esau' heart would not have softened if Jacob had not prevailed in prayer. Jacob acted this way because he did not understand the spiritual dimension of human conflicts so he tried to appease Esau because he was ignorant of the real enemy.

You may be wondering how you may appease the devil. This is how. Some of you may have unbelieving or even, sadly, believing husbands or wives who are difficult. Moreover, you have been straining yourself to love them and might have been compromising your Christian principles thinking that you will win their love by doing so. You have done everything but they have refused to change. The reason is that you have only been trying to appease them.

Perhaps your coworker or boss has made your workplace challenging, tempting you to compromise your morals or engage in unethical behavior to fit in. Or maybe your neighbor harbors resentment toward you, despite your efforts to be kind and courteous, which have proven ineffective. The root issue is that these attempts at appeasement fall short in addressing the spiritual battle at play.

Let me pause to emphasize that when facing a challenging relationship—whether at home, work, or in your neighborhood—first ensure you are not contributing to the problem. *It is tempting to assume your own innocence, but we are all imperfect, and, most times, no one is ever entirely blameless in a conflict.* While one person may bear more responsibility, both parties typically play a role in relational breakdowns. In spiritual warfare, as Sun Tzu wisely noted, victory requires knowing both your enemy and yourself.

Continuing, *human beings sometimes do not act or speak of their own accord.* Either they act in concert with demons or demons are influencing them. Therefore, until you deal with the demons behind their behaviors and actions, you will not have a breakthrough.

If all you do is to just try to love them and be good to them, and you do not confront the enemy behind, you are merely appeasing your enemy. It will not work. They will not change their bad behaviors or cease their hostilities.

Earlier in chapter four of this book, when I explained Jesus' statement *"Do not resist an evil person"*—Matthew 5:39, I said that the Lord was saying do not resist the human counterpart of evil but the demonic counterpart behind the human. Jesus wants us to recognize and confront the evil power behind the human agent or action.

Later in verse 44 of Matthew chapter 5, Jesus says, " . . . *love your enemies and pray for those who persecute you"*—(NIV). Notice that Jesus says to *love* but also to *pray* for our enemies. One powerful prayer is to ask God to free them from the demonic forces driving their actions. What this says is that we must combine loving them with resisting (in prayers) the evil spirits behind them. If you do not do it this way, you will not succeed in ending their hostilities. You will only be appeasing the devil, and you can never appease him. The devil is our determined enemy.

Is there someone you have been trying to win over or get through to? You can break down the invisible wall of hostility by subduing the evil power behind the hostility and you will succeed. You may have to persist for some time, but you will succeed.

After Jacob prevailed in prayers over the demons motivating and influencing Esau, Esau accepted Jacob's gifts—Genesis 33:10–11. Your husband or wife, or boss, or colleague, or neighbor will also respond to and receive your love after you have prevailed over the demonic enemy behind their actions. When you combine the power of loving them and the power of prayer, your human enemies will lay down their arms. This is an unbeatable combination.

PART III. POWER IN YOUR MOUTH

DEFEAT BY SIN

To succeed in spiritual warfare, one critical truth is essential: your prayers must be rooted in a life free from unconfessed sin. This is a foundational requirement for effective prayer. Before you pray, ensure no sin remains that the devil could use against you or as a hold on you.

In Matthew 5:23–24, Jesus teaches that if you're offering a gift at the altar and recall that a brother or sister holds something against you, leave your gift and go make peace with them first. In the Old Testament, the altar was where people met God through sacrifice and prayer. For New Testament believers, our heart is our altar, as Jesus said, *"God is Spirit, and those who worship Him must worship in spirit and truth"* (John 4:24, NKJV). We connect with God through our hearts and spirits. Matthew 5:22 makes it clear that Jesus was describing a case where you have wronged a brother or sister by your words or actions, stressing the need to set things right. Jesus is indicating that unconfessed sins can block our prayers from being effective. Apostle James also says:

> *... The effective, fervent prayer of a righteous man avails much*
> James 5:16 (NKJV)

> *... The prayer of a righteous person is powerful and effective*
> (NIV)

> *... The earnest prayer of a righteous person has great power and produces wonderful results* (NLT)

The prayer of a righteous man or woman avails or is effective. That prayer makes tremendous power available and produces wonderful results.

You may have been wondering why your prayers are not getting the results you hope for. Perhaps, the devil has a hold on you. If you are living in sin or hiding unconfessed sin, your prayers will not break through. In John 14, Jesus spoke to His disciples about His coming death. In verse 29, He says, " *... for the ruler of this world [the devil] is coming, and he has nothing in Me*" (NKJV) or *"For the prince of this world is coming. He has no hold over me ... "* (NIV). Jesus is explaining that the devil will play a role in His death, but not because he has any claim or evidence of sin against Him, as in a court case. He was going to die because it was His mission. This means that the devil has no dirt on Jesus—no sin, weakness, or accusation he can use to control or defeat Him but it also shows that the devil can have power over us if we harbor unconfessed or unrepented sin in our lives.

Jacob's story illustrates this struggle. In Genesis 32, he wrestled with the angel—a picture of prayer—but had not broken through by daybreak. It was not that he needed to pray for hours; Jesus warned against long, repetitive prayers like those of pagans who think they impress God with their many words (Matthew 6:7, NIV). Jacob's delay in victory was because the devil had a grip on him, hindering his breakthrough. The answer to his "prayers" was delayed because of a sin from before.

Twenty years before, Jacob had tricked his brother Esau out of his birthright and deceived their father, Isaac, to steal Esau's blessing. The devil, aware of these sins, used them to fuel Esau's anger, aiming to destroy Jacob. Scripture says that the devil is " . . . *the accuser of our brethren*" Revelation 12:10. He exploits the wrongs in our lives to accuse and attack us.

Let me say a few things about justification. It is because we have been justified through the death and resurrection of Jesus Christ that the devil can no longer accuse us except we have an unconfessed or an un-repented sin in our lives. Justification is what frees us from the accusations of the devil in the court of Heaven. We previously saw how Satan (the devil) accused Joshua, the High Priest before God in the book of Zechariah chapter 3:1–5. The Lord intervened and rebuked Satan.

Justification through the blood of Jesus is what gives us the spiritual legal ground to stand in battle against the devil and prevail. The Bible says that *"And they overcame him by the blood of the Lamb . . . "*—Revelations 12:11 (NKJV).

Apostle Paul was also making this point when he said in Romans 8:37 " . . . *we are more than conquerors through him who loved us."* However, prior to this, he said in verse 33 *"Who will bring any charge against those whom God has chosen? It is God who justifies."* Paul is saying that justification is the basis for our victory. It is the basis for us being more than conquerors as it is said in Revelations *"And they overcame him by the blood of the Lamb."*

You might have sinned years ago, maybe even decades back. However, if you have not truly repented or confessed that sin, the devil still has a hold on you.

I heard this story of a Christian couple who before they were married, were living in fornication, having sexual relations, while they were dating. 5 years after they had been married, they had no children. All that while, they were praying and trusting God but nothing happened. It was not until they confessed this sin and properly repented of it before a minister, to whom God had revealed the sin, that their deliverance or breakthrough came.

This may be the reason why your own deliverance has not come. Some of the problems you now have may be because of a sin or sins in your past of which you need to repent of properly. The Bible says:

> *Therefore confess your sins to each other and pray for each other so that you may be healed.*
> James 5:16a (NIV)

Until you confess that sin, your healing will not appear. It may be that the reason that you are having problems getting pregnant or that you are having problems with your finances or business is because of an unconfessed sin. You need to confess the sin to the right person who can pray for you so that you may be healed.

Past sins, whether committed by believers or non-believers, carry consequences many do not grasp. Scripture teaches that we reap what we sow (Galatians 6:7). Apostle Paul wrote this to the Galatians—believers. This means that the principle of reaping what we sow applies not just to unbelievers but to Christians too. As believers, we know Jesus forgives our past when we accept Him, and that is true. Yet, we often overlook that the fallout from a wrong we did to someone or a sin from our past can still show up, like a harvest we did not expect. A Christian minister said, "*We do not reap in the same season that we sow.*" Therefore, we often forget what we did in the past and fail to see that a present difficulty may be because of something in our past. Our past may be affecting our present.

The past is done before God but the devil may use it as a hold against us if we have not repented of it or confessed the sin. Earlier in my Christian faith, the Lord put it on my heart to apologize to people that I wronged in the past and I wrote them to apologize.

I understand that making things right may not always be possible, especially if you cannot reach the person you wronged. In such cases, confess the sin to God and seek His forgiveness. If admitting a past wrong could lead to legal trouble, ask the Lord for guidance. If He leads you to confess to the person, follow His will. Otherwise, confessing to God and asking for His forgiveness is enough. Trust that God will give you wisdom and grace to move forward.

Getting back to Jacob, God knew of these sins in his life and God could not help him against Esau until Jacob confessed those sins. Even though God had given Jacob angelic escorts, Genesis 32:1–2 says, "*Jacob also went on his way, and the angels of God met him,"* God could not intervene. The angels were not going to be able to help or defend him until Jacob confessed his sins.

God was obligated to protect Jacob because of the covenant He had with him—Genesis chapter 28. Therefore, God brought him to the place of prayer so that He may get Jacob to confess his sins. However, Jacob would not. The Bible says in Genesis 32:25:

> *When the man [the angel] saw that he could not overpower him,*
> *he touched the socket of Jacob's hip*
> *so that his hip was wrenched as he wrestled with the man.*

God wanted Jacob to confess his sin, but Jacob resisted. Genesis 32:25 notes that the angel could not overpower him. You might be praying for a breakthrough or deliverance, yet God may be calling you to address a sin in your life. Victory will not come until you take the first step of confessing that sin. You may need to repent or admit it to someone. Until you do, no matter how long or hard you pray, your prayers will lack power, and you will not overcome the forces of darkness.

The Bible says, *"My spirit shall not always strive with man"*—Genesis 6:3. Therefore, in verse 26 when it was already daybreak, the angel asked that Jacob should let him go. Nevertheless, Jacob wanted the blessing and did not let the angel go. Therefore, the angel said, *" . . . What is your name?"*—verse 27 (NKJV). To paraphrase, what the angel was saying when he asked his name is this, "I cannot bless you unless you acknowledge your sins." Jacob seemed to understand this, so he answered "Jacob."

The name "Jacob" literally means "supplanter." The Free Dictionary defines supplanter as *"one who wrongfully or illegally seizes and holds the place of another."* Jacob was a usurper, had craftily seized Esau's birthright and with the instigation and connivance of their mother Rebecca, he had taken Esau's blessings. This does not in any way absolve Esau of his godlessness, as the Bible calls it in Hebrews 12:16 (NIV), but Jacob had wronged him and needed to make things right before God.

By saying his name, Jacob owned up. He was saying, "Yes, I am a supplanter, a cheat and a deceiver." He was acknowledging his sins against his father and brother. The moment Jacob confessed, God flipped the script on the devil. He yanked the ground out from under Satan's feet and declared Jacob righteous. The battle was settled—Jacob was the winner.

The angel declared, *"Your name will no longer be Jacob, but Israel"* (Genesis 32:28, NIV). God wiped away Jacob's past, proclaiming him not guilty. The devil lost any ground to hold Jacob's sins against him or accuse him in Heaven's court. Jacob triumphed over Satan and his demonic forces. Immediately, God's angels, who had been with Jacob all along, sprang into action. They routed the forces of darkness and put them to flight.

You may have prayed long and hard like Jacob, yet still not broken through. Like Jacob, you might need to come clean before God. Sincere repentance could be the key. The sin holding you back might be a wrong you did to someone, as Jacob wronged his father and Esau. You may need to repent or even make things right with them, what the Bible calls restitution.

Remember the story of Zacchaeus, the tax collector, in Luke chapter 19. As soon as he made commitments to make restitution to those he had cheated, Jesus said to him:

> *Today salvation has come to this house,*
> *because this man, too, is a son of Abraham*
> Verse 9 (NIV)

Your salvation will come too, when you confess and acknowledge your sins to God. As long as you are unwilling to do this, you will continue to pray in vain. If you want to prevail in spiritual warfare, you must be sure that the devil has nothing on you and in you.

You cannot be a cheat, fornicator, adulterer, a taker of bribes, etc. and expect to win against the powers of darkness. You will only " . . . *be ready to punish every act of disobedience, once your own obedience is complete*" — 2 Corinthians 10:6.

I pray that you go forward from this moment and start walking in your God given freedom. I urge you to read this book as often as needed until you have absorbed its truth. Remember that as you start taking a stand and fighting for the victory and freedom that you have in Christ, the forces of darkness that might have oppressed or opposed you until now, will not go down quietly, but you must also persist and resist.

In the temptation of Jesus in Matthew chapter 4, the devil did not leave Jesus after the first and second times, it was only after the third time that he departed. Be assured that the devil will similarly fail in your life and he will have no choice but to depart. The Bible says, " . . . *resist the devil and he will flee from you*" James 4:7. May God bless you!